Of

Angels

and

Miracles:

Faith

Of Angels and Miracles: Faith

By Felix F. Giordano

Red Road Publishers

Ashford, Connecticut

Also by

Felix F. Giordano

The Jim Buchanan Novels:

Montana Harvest

Mystery at Little Bitterroot

The Killing Zone

Missing in Montana

Miracle of the Talking Stick

For more information go to:

jbnovels.com

Publisher's Note: This is a work of fiction. Names, characters, places, and incidents either are a product of the author's imagination or used in a purely fictitious manner. Any resemblance to actual persons living or dead, business establishments, events or locales are purely coincidental.

Published in the United States by Red Road Publishers, PO Box 460 Ashford, CT—www.redroadpublishers.com

Copyright ©2019, 2020 by Felix F. Giordano

Second Edition 2020

All Rights Reserved

No part of this book may be reproduced, scanned, or distributed in any printed or electronic form for public or private use—other than for "fair use" as brief quotations embodied in articles and reviews––without the prior written permission of the publisher.

Of Angels and Miracles: Faith

ISBN: 978-1-950206-02-5

Reg. No., U.S. Copyright Office: TXu 2-132-779

Library of Congress Control Number: 2020925704

Printed in the United States of America

Available at Amazon.com

10 9 8 7 6 5 4 3 2

For Bette

Because Angels and Miracles

are part of who you are

Of Angels and Miracles: Faith

TABLE OF CONTENTS

The Lost Relics of Mount Quarantania   Pg 1

Forever Without End   Pg 27

In My Life   Pg 57

Union Station Angel   Pg 69

Six-winged shapeshifters who patrol the galaxy, leaving a vapor trail of heavenly fragrance in their wake –

John Milton, Paradise Lost

The Lost Relics of Mount Quarantania

Do we ever really consider how events on this Earth transpired? Do we ever look at gaps in the historical record and wonder, what if?

The racing Jeep Wrangler braked hard. The driver leaped from the vehicle as a particle-laden gust of arid wind ripped the brown felt fedora from his head.

He ignored his fallen hat and instead struggled with the odd-shaped burlap bag under his arm. He leaned his body onto the driver's door and closed it with a thud. After he righted himself, he stopped to look at his wife in the passenger seat.

"Don't worry Carmela, I'll be safe."

"Oh Aaron," she moaned. She then dropped her head onto her open palms.

He stared at her for a long moment, his thoughts journeyed to a time when they were both healthy, and shared memorable excursions.

A chartered cruise circumnavigating Kauaʻi Hawaiʻi, a Buddhist pilgrimage to Śrī Laṃkā, a winter's rental in Mývatn Iceland where they witnessed the Aurora Borealis' spontaneous nightly dance evolve across the northern sky, and finally a once in a lifetime summer field trip to remote, far northwestern Montana to explore the Yaak wilderness habitat of the mighty grizzly bear and participate in an environmental field study.

Aaron returned to reality and then abruptly turned away from the driver's side window. He sprinted up the museum's marble steps, opened the massive front door, and walked inside. A receptionist with an olive complexion greeted him. Aaron noticed her black slacks, black robe, red, orange, and white shawl complemented by a black and red head scarf.

"Welcome to the Jericho Museum of Natural History," The woman said.

"Thanks." Aaron looked around. "Where's your curator?"

"He is busy."

Aaron held the burlap bag at arm's length. "He must see this."

The receptionist gathered a pad and pencil from her desk drawer. "I can schedule you to see him. What day is good for you?"

Aaron shouted. "I must see him now!"

"I'm sorry but…"

"Now," Aaron yelled.

The woman picked up her phone and spoke in Arabic. As quickly as she hung up, from a side door, a hefty, bearded man, dressed in tailored gray slacks and a crisp blue polo shirt emerged. He rushed up to Aaron.

"Who are you and why are you here?" the man demanded as his hands settled on his hips.

Aaron smiled. "I have something important to show you."

The man asked, "You are American, no? Always no time to wait, you people let the world fly by and never grasp its beauty."

Aaron smiled. "What I have to show you will change the world forever."

"What is so important? I am Juhaym Razam, the museum curator. Now tell me, how can I help you?"

"My name is Aaron Cohen. I'm Assistant Professor of Anthropology at Columbia University in New York. I'm in Jordan visiting with my wife and…"

"Where is your wife?" Mister Razam asked.

Aaron lost his train of thought. "My wife? Why…well, she's in the car."

Mister Razam glanced through the front door's glass windows. "Please ask her to come inside," he said. "A woman should not sit in a hot automobile. It is my honor and responsibility as a host to welcome her."

Aaron first hesitated and then responded. "My wife is not well. She has trouble walking."

Mister Razam took a step toward the front door. "Then, I will assist her."

Aaron spoke with a loud voice, "No, she uses a cane. It's very painful for her to move more than necessary. It's best that she stays restful and remains still."

Mister Razam stopped in his tracks, turned and stared at Aaron. Then he said, "I'm sorry for her. Please tell her for me that I will mention her plight in Friday's prayers. But in this world perhaps we can help. My sister happens to be a physical therapist and my brother is a neurologist. Upon my insistence, I know they would be pleased to assist with your wife's recovery while you are guests in our country."

Aaron replied, "You don't understand. For several years now, my wife's body has been ravaged by an incurable illness. We've been to so many doctors. It seems as if the progression of her illness has stalled for the moment, but eventually she will die, every doctor has given her a terminal prognosis. But that's something we've grown to live with."

"Mister Cohen, I am truly sorry for your wife. We must waste no time so that you can be back with her. Now, what can I do for you?"

"I found an artifact in the desert." Aaron handed the curator the burlap bag. "I need you to look at this item and verify its significance. I believe it will surpass the Seven Wonders of the Ancient World, collectively."

Mister Razam peeked inside the bag and gazed at the artifact for a long moment. His eyes then met Aaron's and he stared at him. Mister Razam then cleared his throat and looked down at the bag.

Without turning his head, he looked out of the corner of his eye at the receptionist, and said, "Jana, please lock the front doors and then contact security and have them immediately escort all visitors out of the building."

The receptionist directly got up from behind her desk and made a beeline for the front doors. She pulled a cellphone from her pocket and then Aaron overheard her speak into the phone.

"Sergeant Haddad, Curator Razam has issued a Code Red, I repeat, a Code Red. Coordinate a full building evacuation without delay."

Mister Razam then waved Aaron into his office. "Come with me."

"What's going on?" Aaron asked.

"Silence. Just come with me."

The curator closed the door behind them and placed the bag on his desk. He gazed at Aaron and then dug deep into the satchel. He carefully removed the rolled-up scroll from inside the burlap sack.

Aaron could not control his enthusiasm. As his hands

shook, he said, "I believe it's from the first century."

Instantly, a weak, sarcastic belly laugh escaped from Mister Razam after Aaron's comment. "Mister Cohen, your optimism is commendable. However, don't be so optimistic. The desert ages things beyond their years. Where did you find this?"

Aaron said, "The Mount of Temptation."

"Mount Quarantania?" Mister Razam asked.

Aaron nodded. "Well, yes...in a cave on that mountain."

Mister Razam partially unraveled the scroll with great care so as not to damage it. He pulled out a magnifying glass, sat in his red leather chair, and with his face up close began to study the artifact. After a few minutes, he stared at Aaron. "It is in Aramaic. It is written on papyrus."

Aaron nodded to himself. "I translated the first few words, can you decipher the rest?"

Mister Razam continued to read the transcript. After examining the scroll for nearly a half-hour, he then stopped and placed the magnifying glass down. "I need help...someone to decode it."

"Who?" Aaron asked.

With much care, Mister Razam placed the scroll back into the bag. Then he said, "This museum has experts in the field of archaic languages and antiquities. They are in the field right now on a dig in the Sinai, but they will be back next month, and I can have them look at it."

Aaron shook his head. "That's too long to wait. We must return to New York City by next week." Aaron reached for the bag. "I'll go elsewhere."

Mister Razam uttered a guttural laugh, shook his head, and then reached out with one of his meat hook hands and grabbed Aaron's arm as it latched onto the bag. "I am sorry Mister Cohen. We have rules here. This must remain in the museum."

Aaron took a step back. "What do you mean? We're leaving. I can't wait around for months while your experts crawl all over this with their magnifying glasses and million-dollar electron microscopes. Besides, I found it so it's mine!"

Mister Razam laughed. "Oh Mister Cohen, I'm very sorry to say that you are mistaken. It will remain in the Jericho Museum."

"No sir. You can't, you mustn't," Aaron pleaded.

Mister Razam tucked the bag under his arm. "You see Mister Cohen; all artifacts found in Jordan belong to the government. We only release them to the people who discovered them if they are simply found to be innocuous."

Aaron yelled, "What...what kind of policy is that?"

Mister Razam scowled at Aaron. "It is a Jordanian policy. If this is found to be a significant relic, then it will be evaluated as such, catalogued, and then entered into the museum's collection."

Aaron pleaded, "But..."

Mister Razam interrupted him. "That is all, Mister Cohen. Please go now. Have the receptionist let you out. This museum will be closed for the remainder of the day. I will call you tomorrow after I've thoroughly examined this artifact."

"Then I can take it with me?" Aaron asked.

Mister Razam pouted and then returned the scroll to the burlap bag. "I explained to you the situation. If you do not have the patience to wait until we determine what this is then I suggest that you leave Jordan at once and forget that you ever saw this."

Tears welled up in Aaron's eyes. "I plead with you Mister Razam. I need this artifact to help cure my wife. I explained to you how sick she is. If you are a decent Jordanian, please show us some mercy."

Mister Razam pointed his finger at Aaron. "Mister Cohen, as you would say in the United States, do not patronize me...or my country for that matter."

"But..."

"Do not speak an additional word more on this matter. You are fortunate that I promised to contact you once our experts in the field examine this artifact. Go now, Mister Cohen."

Aaron sighed as he watched Mister Razam place the bag in the upper left-hand desk drawer and lock the desk. Frustrated and helpless, Aaron gave Mister Razam his business card. On the back of the card, Aaron inscribed the name of the local hotel and the room number where they were staying. When Aaron returned to his Jeep he saw Carmela in the passenger seat with the door open as the sun shone on her ankle-length, white chiffon dress.

Aaron said, "Carmela, I'm sorry. I spent too much time in there."

"That's fine Aaron. The warmth of the sun feels good on

my legs."

Aaron said, "Carmela let me tell you what happened in there."

After Aaron finished detailing to Carmela the entire event inside the museum, she asked, "Can they do that?"

Aaron conceded, "Apparently but I'm going to stay on top of this. If that artifact is what I think it is, and they let us keep it, it will change our lives forever. We'll finally have the money for your operation."

Aaron drove to the hotel, parked the Jeep, and walked to the passenger side. He opened the door and lifted Carmela out of her seat. She put down a wooden cane and limped along as she leaned her right arm on Aaron's shoulder for support.

Aaron practically carried her up to their room and gently placed her on the bed. They spent the next few hours talking about their adventure on Mount Quarantania.

"You seemed to be walking better, Carmela." Aaron stated as he sat on a club chair that faced the bed.

Carmela lamented, "Oh Aaron, my leg is getting worse."

"Then why were you smiling when we were at the find?" Aaron asked.

Carmela smiled. "Oh Aaron, it was the adrenalin rush from the excitement of the discovery. The pain is still there."

Aaron said, "Don't worry, we'll find you a cure. I won't let this illness consume you."

Carmela pleaded, "Aaron, I'm so weary from the dozens of doctor appointments and the many flights from one city to another hoping to find a cure. Even though I can't do what I love anymore and I'm in constant pain, to helplessly pursue treatments full of false hopes and promises are just simply cruel. I'm not putting up with it any longer."

Carmela lay on the bed with her head propped up on two pillows. Patches of dark skin on her shin, a manifestation of her disease, contrasted with her Mediterranean complexion as her crooked and shortened right leg lay in plain view.

Aaron got up from the chair and walked over to the bed. "Please Carmela, give me one last chance. The sale of this artifact will provide us with the money so that we won't have to rely on second-rate hospitals and doctors in training. We'll get the best medical care for you."

Carmela said, "The doctors we've seen say they can't cure the fibrous dysplasia, and neither can the doctors they've studied under. So nothing really matters anymore, does it?"

Aaron replied, "It's not those doctors. It's the money that will find you the very best doctor who will operate."

"Aaron, there's no cure. Can't you get it through your head? They might as well have amputated my leg. Your life would be so much happier if I went back to *Napoli* to live with *mia Madre*." Carmela broke into tears.

Aaron sat on the bed and hugged Carmela. "I love you and I'll do anything for you. We'll get help."

They lay on the bed in each other's arms. A few minutes later they fell asleep from exhaustion. An hour later a knock at the door woke them up.

Aaron sat up in bed. "Yes, who is it?"

A voice from the hallway boomed, "Chief Maloof of the Jericho Police, please open the door."

Aaron jumped off the bed, put his ear to the door, and asked, "What is it?"

"Please open the door now," Chief Maloof said.

Aaron complied and found himself facing a large man in full uniform wearing a sidearm. His black hair, framed by a mustache that seemed to span from one cheek to the other, was marked by a multitude of curls.

"What can I do for you?" Aaron asked.

"I am Basil Maloof, Chief of the Jericho Police. Are you the American, Mister Aaron Cohen?"

Aaron responded, "Yes, what is this about?"

"You found the scroll?" Chief Maloof looked past Aaron at Carmela's twisted position on the bed.

"Yes, I'm Professor Cohen. I'm an Assistant Professor of Anthropology at Columbia University in New York." A flash of anger flew through Aaron's head and he decided to impress the local man. "I'm also Chief Archeologist at the New York Museum of Natural History."

Chief Maloof blinked his eyes slowly. "I'm sorry Mister Cohen. The scroll has been surrendered to our government. I am here to inform you that your business in Jericho has ended and you must leave at once."

Aaron flinched and then said, "What...leave? But I found

that scroll. It belongs to me."

"No sir, it belongs to our government. You have until tomorrow morning to leave Jericho. If you do not comply you will be arrested at noon. Good day, Mister Cohen."

The police chief turned and left. The hallway resounded with the clickety-clack resonance of Chief Basil Maloof's black Belleville boots hitting the floor. When he descended the hallway and stepped out of the view of the Cohen's hotel room, Aaron shut the door and turned to his wife.

"See Carmela, they know what it is. If they didn't, they wouldn't be trying to kick us out of the country. I know what this is, they can't fool me, and they won't so help me God."

"Aaron, forget about it. It's just scribbling."

Aaron walked to the window and looked down at the street. "No Carmela, it's anything but scribbling. I'm going to get it back." He turned to face her. "It's our ticket to fortune."

"Aaron, don't you dare. Please come to bed."

He took a step toward the bed and then stopped in mid-stride. "I've got to settle down. The police chief's got me haywired. I'm going down to the lobby. They serve traditional Bedouin coffee with aromatic green cardamom. Would you like me to bring a cup upstairs for you?"

Carmela settled in the bed and pulled the sheet up to her neck. "No thank you, Aaron. I'm so tired. Please take the key to the room with you. I'll be asleep when you get back."

Aaron grabbed the key off the nightstand as Carmella curled up in bed. He left the room and then walked down the stairs as a tingling sensation flowed through his entire body. When he reached the lobby, he spotted a man at the front desk.

"Hello Mister Cohen, may I help you?" asked the night manager.

Aaron stared at the man for a moment and then said, "Zaid Haddad, correct?"

The night manager stepped out from behind the desk. He wore a blue sport jacket, blue print tie, and khaki pants. "Ah, Mister Cohen, you have a memory for the ages." He laughed and then asked, "I trust the room is satisfactory for you and your wife?"

Aaron replied, "Oh yes, it is. I have no complaints."

"Well then, what can I do for you?" Zaid asked.

"I want to go for a walk but first I would love a cup of your Bedouin coffee."

Zaid smiled. "Mister Cohen, it would be my pleasure to offer you a cup." He went into the back and after a couple of minutes he returned holding a steaming white porcelain coffee cup decorated in a gold leaf design. After he handed it to Aaron he said, "I shall be right back."

"Where are you going?" Aaron asked.

Zaid turned to Aaron and said, "Another guest upstairs, on the floor above you is having difficulty with the lock on their door. I shall be back shortly. If you will still be here, I would like to offer you another cup of coffee and I will join you. I would love to hear about America from, as you say…a local?"

Aaron nodded. "I'll be here. Another cup of coffee would be much appreciated."

He watched Zaid turn and bound up the staircase. After a few minutes, just as he was finishing his first cup of coffee, Aaron heard footsteps come from the backroom. He saw a man emerge from behind a white acrylic beaded curtain. The man wore a beige camelhair sweater over a white dress shirt and a red striped tie. His gray, pleated dress slacks completed his outfit.

"Hello," Aaron said.

The man had a neatly trimmed beard and short hair. He smiled at Aaron. "How do you do sir?"

"I'm fine, how are you?"

"I am well. You are the American, Aaron Cohen?"

"Yes I am."

"And your wife Carmela…how is she?"

Aaron asked with a quizzical look on his face, "How do you know my wife's name?"

The man laughed and then said, "It is my job to know who is in this hotel."

Aaron smiled. "Yes, I suppose it is. She's fine."

The man stepped behind the hotel desk and asked, "How was your business at the museum today? Did you settle your differences with Mister Razam?"

Aaron stepped back. "How do you know about that?"

"The news about your find is all over Jericho."

"It is?" Aaron asked.

The man replied, "Oh yes. Even the little children who play

in the streets know about what you found."

With a slight tilt of his head, Aaron asked, "Who are you?"

The man smiled. "You may call me Shay."

Aaron asked, "Is that your name?"

Shay replied, "A shortened version, most people find that my real name is just much too difficult to pronounce."

Aaron leaned on the front desk. "Tell me, what are the people saying?"

"About what?"

"About what I found."

Shay smiled. "Oh that. No human eyes should ever read it. It is prophesied that whoever finds it must dispose of it."

"Dispose of it, why?" Aaron asked.

Shay leaned forward on the front desk and whispered, "Oh Mister Cohen, there is a curse on that object, and it can only lead to trouble, perhaps even death. They won't tell you that at the museum because they believe it should be delivered to the government. They wish to use it to start a war."

Aaron scoffed, "That's silly. It's a sacred relic."

Shay glared at Aaron and said, "It's not sacred, it's a complete forgery."

"Forgery?" Aaron shrugged. "How can you even say that? Have you no faith in God?"

"Mister Cohen, I am not a believer. There is nothing once this life is over. It's as simple as turning off a light switch. But I do have faith Mister Cohen. I have faith in myself." He whispered in Aaron's ear. "The government wishes to deceive you. Destroy that corrupt evil thing that you found while you have the chance."

Aaron winced. "I can't destroy it."

Shay pleaded with Aaron, "Please get it back from the museum. You know that your intent tonight was to get it back. Bring it to me. I will destroy it for you."

Aaron felt his patience reach a boiling point with Shay when he heard footsteps on the staircase. He turned and saw Zaid descend the stairs. At once Aaron's anger began to dissipate and he knew that Zaid would be a more reasonable source of information.

Zaid said, "Ah, Mister Cohen you did wait for me to return before you go for your walk. Do you still want to have Bedouin coffee with me?"

Aaron said, "Yes, and I'll buy one for your employee."

"What employee?" Zaid asked.

Aaron turned and saw no one where Shay had stood just seconds ago. "He was right here," Aaron said.

"Now who would that be?" Zaid asked.

"Shay."

"Shay who?"

Aaron said, "I don't know his last name, but he had a beard and wore gray pants and a sweater."

Zaid stepped up to Aaron. "No one by that description has been here today and certainly doesn't work for us."

Aaron insisted, "He came through the curtain from your back room."

Zaid stepped past Aaron and stared into the back room. He turned around, faced Aaron, and said, "No one is in there."

"What?" Aaron slipped by Zaid and looked for himself. He turned, started at Zaid, and then said, "But he was with me, right here. Don't you believe me?"

Zaid shook his head. "Dear Mister Cohen, let me get you another cup of coffee. Then you can sit with me for a while. Relax and then get a good night's rest."

Aaron asked, "I suppose that you also want me to destroy what I found."

Zaid stared at Aaron. "Destroy what?"

Aaron replied, "What I found."

"What did you find, Mister Cohen?"

"Everyone knows what I found. Shay said that himself."

Zaid said, "Mister Cohen, there is no one named Shay, and I for one do not know what you found."

Aaron took the coffee cup from Mister Haddad and sat at a table in the lobby. Zaid walked over with a cup of his own and they sat together.

After a few sips, Aaron confided in Zaid of the find on Mount Quarantania and the happenings at the museum. "So much has happened today. Perhaps I was seeing things?" Aaron asked.

Zaid gave Aaron a serious look and said, "Too much time in the desert can do funny things to our minds. I suggest that you get a good night's rest and then tomorrow, discuss your options with the museum."

The two men enjoyed their coffees and engaged in casual conversation. Later that evening, well past midnight, Aaron went back to the room and noticed that Carmela was fast asleep. He grabbed his coat and went downstairs to his Jeep. He reached in the back and pulled out a crow bar.

Aaron walked the two-mile distance to the museum. He was careful to stay off the sidewalks and streets, walking between houses and in dark alleyways. A barking dog caused Aaron to panic. In the darkness, he stumbled into the wall of a building and fell to the ground. He gathered himself and then continued on his way.

When Aaron reached the museum, he peered into one of the windows and saw that no one was inside. Aaron leaned onto the window pane and it immediately shattered. He then slipped into the museum.

He rested his shoulder onto the door of the curator's office and pushed his full weight against the door. When the doorframe shattered Aaron walked inside. He ran to the desk and jiggled the drawer. After a few tries, the drawer opened, and he spotted the burlap bag.

Aaron opened the bag, looked inside, and then examined the scroll to ensure it was still intact. He tucked it under his arm and escaped the way he entered. On the way back to the hotel, Aaron heard a voice call to him.

He turned to look and spotted the silhouette of a man. It was Shay and he ran toward Aaron. In an instant, defying all logic, Shay was upon Aaron and in his face.

"What in hell do you think you're doing with that?" Shay asked.

Aaron stuck the burlap bag higher under his arm, trying to hide it from view. "It's none of your business. Go away and leave me alone."

Shay said, "Mister Cohen, You can't fool me. I know what you have. My nostrils can smell it, my eyes can read it through the bag, and my ears hear those blasphemous words spoken so loudly that it hurts my brain. I've seen that artifact before. It's pure evil and does not deserve the mighty clout you bequeath it. Give it to me. I will see that it receives its rightful fate."

"No," Aaron said.

Shay's eyes bugged forward, and he shouted in a deep,

sharp, and piercing voice from the depths of hell, "Give it to me!"

Aaron yelled back, "You are an archon." Aaron turned and ran, not even looking back. He returned to the hotel room an hour or so before daybreak and awakened Carmela.

"You did what?" she asked.

Aaron was defiant. "It belongs to us. I found it."

"Aaron, you are toying with the supernatural."

"Oh no Carmella, we are in God's good graces for finding this."

She shook her head and then let out an exasperated full breath. "Well then, let me see it."

Aaron stepped toward the bed. When he removed the scroll from the burlap bag, a piece of lined note paper fell onto the comforter. "What's this," he said as he grabbed the paper.

Aaron helped Carmela sit up in bed.

"I want to examine it," she said and put on her reading glasses. She gazed at it for a long moment and then stared at Aaron. When her eyes returned to the paper she said, "It looks Arabic. I still translate for my Lebanese students in New York." Carmela scrutinized it, and then glanced at Aaron. "It seems they were converting the Aramaic to Arabic," she said.

"What does it say?" Aaron asked.

Carmela said, "I'll need more time." She looked toward the desk in the hotel room. "Aaron, get me the pad and pen on the desk."

"Of course," he said and gathered the requested items and brought them to Carmela. "I'm the field archeologist, you're the researcher. Work your magic," Aaron pleaded.

She studied the writing, made notes, then crossed some out, ripped a sheet of paper from the pad, threw it on the floor and then began feverishly writing in earnest.

Carmela glanced at Aaron and said, "There are verses." She read from the translated text. "*My Father hath sent Me. Receive Me for I am the Way, the Truth, and the Light.*" Carmela again looked up at Aaron. "I think..."

Aaron raised his right hand to his face and covered his mouth. "Continue," he said.

Carmela searched the scroll and found other verses. She wrote down the translation and then read aloud. "*It will come to pass that I will spread the Word of My Father to the ends of the*

Earth. I will gather disciples one by one to explain to all of humanity what My Father expects of His people." Carmela looked up at Aaron as a tear rolled down her cheek.

"Go on," Aaron said.

Carmela continued, *"And these disciples, if they so be clean even unto death, shall live for all eternity with Me and I with them. For I seek not worldly riches, nor earthly kingdoms, nor vast armies to rule. My riches will be the souls of men. My Kingdom will be the Heavens above. My armies will be the believers of My Word."*

Aaron stepped away from the bed and said, "Oh my God."

Carmela said, "Wait, that's not all. Listen to these last two verses…*My Word will be the Truth and all who follow My teachings shall be saved. For I have been told this by My Father, your Creator."* Carmela wiped the tears from her face and then stared at her husband. "Aaron, do you know what we have here?"

Aaron replied, "It appears to be the Lost Book of Jesus."

Carmela shook her head and wiped a track of tears from her cheek. "It was just a hypothesis espoused by a factional group of radical biblical archeologists. One of them said he had a vision that told of a papyrus scripture written by the Lord Himself. The theory was that it was written in the Coptic language to prevent its true revelation until the time was right."

"But this is Aramaic not Coptic. Why?" Aaron asked.

Carmela continued, "The premise goes on to say that if it was found earlier, much, much earlier, it would have been deemed unorthodox and even perhaps a fake by the Christian leaders. They wanted to control and centralize their power and anything that would have challenged that power would have had to be destroyed."

Aaron asked, "Even a piece of scripture?"

"Especially a piece of scripture," Carmela said. She presented her opened palms to the artifact. "In lieu of faith and miracles, this artifact wouldn't have stood a chance against early Church leaders whose only concern in life was enhancing their wealth, influence, and power."

Aaron asked, "So from a gnostic perspective, it would have been considered heretical by the Church and destroyed?"

Carmela said, "Even worse, its unearthing in ancient times could have meant death to its discoverer."

Aaron persisted. "But Aramaic, not Coptic like the theory? You haven't answered my question."

Carmela smiled. "I now realize the theory was only half correct."

"What do you mean?" Aaron asked.

Carmela explained, "It was not written in Coptic because it is a dead language. In ancient times, the usage of the Aramaic language continued to expand and in certain areas of the world, in different derivations and forms, it continues to be spoken to this day."

"But why?"

Carmela again smiled. "Now here's my theory. If it was written in Coptic it may never have been understood and certainly not translated. But by it having been written in Aramaic, the Lord knew His words would be recognized even unto today."

Aaron shook his head. "Well, I'll be dammed."

Carmela raised her voice. "Aaron, it's not funny. Don't speak words like that."

"I'm sorry." Aaron sat on the edge of the bed next to Carmela.

She continued, "Christ wrote it when He spent forty days alone in the desert and buried it in a cave on The Mount of Temptation. That's where we discovered it."

"Now I understand that," Aaron said.

Carmela nodded to Aaron. "People often wondered what Christ did, why there was no direct written record of His life prior to His ministry."

Aaron nodded. "So he wrote it hoping that someday someone would come along, find it, and reveal it to the world."

"Exactly. Aaron, we can't keep this."

"Carmela, this is priceless. Just one day at Sotheby's will garner a value high enough to pay for your operation. It could fetch at least eight figures or more. The money that will be left over will make us multimillionaires. We'll write books about this, we'll be on TV, perhaps even have our own cable series on the History Channel or NatGeo." Then Aaron's voice grew hard and coarse. "Don't let it out of your sight."

Carmela responded, "Aaron, there are more important things in life than stealing this religious artifact."

Aaron snapped back, "We're not stealing what we

rightfully found. It will make us rich beyond our imagination."

Carmela shook her head. "So, tell me Aaron, for what?"

Aaron stared at Carmela. "For the operation you need so that you can walk again...so that you can lead a normal life."

"Aaron, I don't want anything to happen to you. We have a good life now. My love for you is more important than being able to walk again. If you get arrested for stealing this, our life as we know it would end."

Aaron ignored Carmela's last few words. "I need to formulate an escape plan. We're getting out of here before they discover it's missing." Aaron looked outside. The hot Jordanian morning sun was already full over the eastern horizon. "I'll bring our luggage to the Jeep. Keep that scroll hidden. I'll help you dress when I come back to the room."

Carmela shook her head and sighed. She slipped the scroll and the brief translation into the burlap bag and stuck it under her bed sheets. She got comfortable in bed and covered herself with the comforter. Aaron busied himself packing their luggage.

He then turned to Carmela, told her he'd be right back, carried their two suitcases into the hallway, and closed the bedroom door behind him. He picked up the suitcases and then felt a tap on his shoulder.

"Mister Cohen, where do you think you're going?"

Startled, Aaron dropped the suitcases and stared in the direction where the voice came from. It was Shay and he had a stern look on his face.

"I'm uh, bringing these to the car. Our dirty laundry is inside these suitcases."

Shay snarled, "Oh, Mister Cohen. I do appreciate your lying but if you must lie, then please make it more believable."

Aaron confronted Shay. "I think I know who you are. What do you want?"

Shay smiled while massaging his chin. He put his hand on Aaron's upper arm and took him aside. Aaron felt a shiver erupt in his arm where Shay touched him and then it sizzled as it traversed throughout his body. With his back against the wall, Aaron shoved Shay away, picked up the suitcases, and ran downstairs. When he reached the lobby, he saw the curator, the Chief of the Jericho Police and another policeman waiting for him.

"Where are you going Professor Cohen?" asked the curator, Juhaym Razam.

Aaron pointed at the Chief of the Jericho Police, Basil Maloof and explained. "He told me that I had to leave today and I'm doing just that right now."

Aaron tried to walk past them, but Chief Maloof interjected. "A few questions first, Mister Cohen. Where were you last night?"

Aaron began to perspire. "I was uh; I was sleeping in my room."

"Who can verify that?" Chief Maloof asked.

Aaron said, "My wife. Why, what's wrong?"

Chief Maloof first glanced at Mister Razam and then at Aaron. "It seems the museum was broken into last night and something was stolen. Something was stolen that you claim to have found yesterday on Mount Quarantania. It seems this is a strange coincidence."

The perspiration fully erupted across Aaron's forehead and he began to fumble with his words. "I, uh, yes I found something. I did find something but, but the last time that I saw it…it was in his office." Aaron pointed at Mister Razam.

"But it is missing now!" Mister Razam glared at Aaron. "He has it."

Chief Maloof instructed his policeman on duty to take Aaron's luggage back upstairs where they would perform a complete inspection of the room and the couple's belongings. Aaron swallowed hard and complied with Chief Maloof.

Just as they reached the second-floor landing, they heard a loud thud inside the room.

Aaron asked, "Carmela, are you all right in there?"

From inside they heard Carmela scream and then say, "Aaron come here quickly."

Aaron clutched the doorknob, but it was hot to the touch. He drew his hand away in pain and then put his fingers to his lips. Aaron stared at Chief Maloof. "Hurry, I believe a demon is in there doing who knows what to my wife."

Chief Maloof quickly grabbed the pair of tactical gloves off the glove clip on his belt and pulled them on. He gripped the doorknob, but the door forcibly swung open seemingly under its own power and slammed against the wall. The four men took a step back. Carmela stood in the middle of the room, her summer pajama shorts revealing the straightness of her leg and the absence of its discoloration and shortness. She stared at Aaron with the scroll in her hand.

"Carmela!" Aaron screamed.

Carmela wept and then said, "Aaron something, I can't, I can't explain has happened. After you left, the bed grew warm, so I threw off the sheets. Then this feeling entered my leg, stretching it, making me feel like I haven't felt since I was a young girl. My leg slowly straightened all by itself. Then the discoloration in my leg began to disappear right before my eyes. I felt the mattress rise and a glow enveloped the room. An orb rose from the floor until it hovered above my bed. Then a voice beckoned me to get up, to get out of bed." Carmela began to cry. "So, I did and I, I walked out of bed, on my own." She looked down at her legs and cried. "Look at me; I haven't walked on my own in two years."

Chief Maloof, Mister Razam, and the other policeman knelt and prayed in Arabic. When Aaron heard them, he turned, and saw their reaction. He reached for Carmela to hug her and felt a sensation like he had never experienced before. It was as if an electrical impulse surged through his entire body and through his extremities. A sense of pure love ebbed and flowed deep within his being while he hung tight onto Carmela.

Full of tears, Aaron said, "Oh Carmela, I love you so much."

"I love you too Aaron." Carmela hugged Aaron and buried her head on his shoulder.

Aaron turned to the others. "You do realize what this is, don't you?"

Chief Maloof got up off his knees and was the first to speak. "Mister Cohen, we all know what this is. I will make sure that it is protected."

When the other policeman got to his feet, Aaron responded, "No, this is the actual Book of Jesus. I must take it with me. The significance of this find needs to be articulated to the entire world."

Mister Razam ended his prayers and stood up. "The scroll must be honored with respect. It cannot be dispatched to…"

Carmela interrupted him and as she wiped her tears she said, "With all due respect, sir, seeing that this has cured me of my disease; it proves that this scroll belongs to all peoples and must not be hidden away inside a museum."

"The madam is correct," said Chief Maloof. "This is the Almighty's blessing. I have jurisdiction over the relic. It must be shared with all religions and does not belong to any one."

Aaron dropped his head, covered his forehead with his left hand, and raised his right palm. "Just wait a minute here." He straightened up, turned to Chief Maloof, and smirked. "Listen, I found this. It belongs to my wife and me."

Chief Maloof shook his head. "No, this is a gift from Allah and Jehovah."

Aaron insisted, "I understand that but let me bring it to the proper authorities."

Mister Razam spoke up. "Chief Maloof is correct. His brother is Mullah of Jericho and I have friends in Jerusalem. One is a Rabbi and the other is the Israeli tourism minister. We will speak with them."

Chief Maloof added, "Yes, I will tell them what I have seen with my own eyes. All religions will have a voice in this matter before anyone decides what should become of it."

"Are you sure that everyone will cooperate?" Aaron asked.

Chief Maloof nodded. "We have witnessed a miracle today. I assure you that I will lay down my life to protect this spiritual relic. It is a direct link with our Creator." He pointed to Carmela. "Her cured affliction is proof of that."

Aaron placed the scroll into the burlap bag and handed it to Chief Maloof. The police chief nodded, thanked Aaron and Carmela and then left. Mister Razam apologized to the couple and told them that not only would he not be pressing charges but that he wanted no compensation for the damage to the museum.

Aaron and Carmela decided to leave that same day. After packing their luggage in the Jeep, Aaron drove to the Jericho Museum. They sat inside the Jeep and reflected on everything that had happened.

With his hands on the steering wheel and looking at the front doors of the museum, Aaron laughed. "What an amazing adventure, and to think that we actually touched something that the Lord created."

Carmela smiled. "Aaron, have faith. Every day we touch something the Lord has made." She leaned over, held his face in her hands, and kissed him.

Aaron touched the moistness on his cheek where Carmela's lips had been. "It's been so long since you've done that."

"Aaron, we'll have a wonderful rest of our life together. It's a true wonder what the Lord has done for us. Letting us find that scroll, driving us toward the healing of my illness. I can't seem to comprehend the magnitude of it all. Are you sorry that you don't have the scroll anymore?"

Aaron glanced at Carmela. "No, I have you and you're well again. I'd trade a rolled-up scroll for a miracle any day."

"Are you sure?" Carmella asked.

Aaron smiled. "I'm sure. Besides, the scroll will go where it belongs. To be shared with the world."

"No regrets?"

"None." Aaron reached into his pocket and pulled out a long, thin burlap bag. "We still have this."

"What's that, Aaron?"

"When I found that burlap bag with the scroll inside, I also found this." Aaron unraveled the bag revealing a thin reed pen broken in a half-dozen pieces.

"Aaron what is that?"

"Carmela, I think this is the pen Christ used to write his words on the scroll."

"Aaron, if it is, it belongs with the scroll."

"Carmela, we will deliver this directly to the Israeli Tourism Minister and explain everything to him. This will ensure that they both end up together where they rightfully belong."

"Are you sure that's the right thing to do?" Carmela asked.

Aaron gazed into Carmela's eyes. "Last night on my way to the museum I was startled by a dog tied in the backyard of one of the houses. It was dark and, in the confusion, I dropped the crowbar. I still ran to the museum, but I knew I couldn't get inside. That's when I removed the bag with the reed pen and held it up to my face to look at it. I was outside the museum near one of the windows and the glass pane shattered on its own. I climbed through the window frame and into the museum. I walked up to the door to the curator's office. With the bag in my hand I felt around for a place to pry the door open with my fingers. When the bag touched the door, the door frame broke by itself and the door swung open. When I got to the curator's desk, I placed the bag against the drawer and the drawer popped open. I found the crowbar on my way back to the hotel. I placed it on the backseat of the Jeep."

"Aaron?"

"Carmela, the scroll and the reed pen will find their way, they belong together." Aaron placed the reed pen back in the bag and held it on his lap.

"Are you sure?"

"Carmela dear, have faith."

When Aaron started the engine, he felt Carmela touch his arm. "Aaron, let me drive. It's been so long since I was able to."

Aaron agreed and they swapped seats. A few miles outside of town, Aaron caught a glimpse of a blur by the side of the road. Then he noticed that Carmela pulled the car off to the shoulder of the road.

"Carmela, why are we stopping?" Aaron asked.

"Oh Aaron, I saw this poor man hitchhiking. After our experience, I've learned that we need to share our good fortune with others."

"What man?"

Carmela said, "A bearded man. He wore a sweater, a red tie, and a pair of gray slacks."

Aaron placed the bag with the reed pen in the glove compartment and reached in back for the crowbar. He got out, slammed shut the passenger door and ran to the man.

Shay greeted Aaron. "Mister Cohen, I'm glad you decided to listen to me. Although you no longer have the scroll, I will be glad to accept that reed pen from you. Then I will no longer bother you."

Aaron raised the crowbar above his head. "Shay, go back to the depths from where you came."

Shay shrugged his shoulders and said, "I know not of what you speak."

Aaron yelled, "I know who you are. I denounce you Satan, just as the Lord rejected you two-thousand years ago. I command you to return to Hell and to never return to tempt or harass my wife and me ever again."

When Shay's face began to distort into a misshapen image, Aaron swung the crowbar and leveled it across Shay's face. Shay's form burst into a flash of fire that faded in an instant and an unearthly howl echoed in the oppressive desert air and then Shay was gone forever.

Aaron returned to the Jeep and dropped the crowbar onto the backseat. He stared at Carmela.

"What happened to the man who was hitchhiking?" Carmela asked.

Aaron laughed, "He's gone."

Carmela looked in her rearview mirror. "You're right. I don't see him anymore. Are you sure he's gone?"

Aaron nodded. "Carmela, have faith. Yes, he's gone. Have faith."

The Fictional Book of Jesus

Found in a Mount Quarantania cave, written in 26 AD

Chapter 1

1.1 My Father hath sent Me.
1.2 Receive Me for I am the Way, the Truth and the Light.
1.3 The Truth shall be known unto you, so that all men may live forever.
1.4 Live in the fruits of thy salvation and let it be known known that salvation is the way of the Lord.
1.5 The Lord hath given you the tools of redemption.
1.6 Refrain not from redemption for it is the way of the light.
1.7 The light will guide you, for it is written that unto all men who shall follow the Truth shall not be once saved but saved for all eternity.
1.8 Those who are saved shall live in everlasting happiness with the Lord.
1.9 For the Lord's House is open to all men who seek and follow the Truth.
1.10 Those who do not follow the Truth shall not see the light.
1.11 For if you do not seek the light, you shall live in darkness and those who dwell in the darkness shall be dammed for all eternity.

The Fictional Book of Jesus
Chapter 2

1.1 And it came to pass that the Shepherd would walk among his flock.
1.2 Speaking to all who would listen, I will gather the good and cast away the evil.
1.3 Those who would listen and were believers would find a place in the House of the Lord.
1.4 For it will be written that some men will refuse to follow My teachings by their own accord.
1.5 Some will influence others to disobey the teachings of the Lord.
1.6 Some will bear weapons against others in the cause of righteousness even unto the Name of the Lord.
1.7 I tell you they are all blasphemers.
1.8 For the Lord would never ask men to sacrifice each other for the sake of God.
1.9 All lives are precious in Mine eyes and only the Lord may decide the fate of all men.
1.10 For what man would strike his own brother at the insistence of his master.
1.11 So, I say unto you, do not strike thy fellow brethren for I and My Father love you all as brothers and children.
1.12 As it is written, that you come from the womb of God.
1.13 A temple so clean, that when you return to God's Home to be judged it is My Father's wish that you shall arrive as clean as when you left.
1.14 He who returns blemished by other men shall be welcomed at the right side of God.
1.15 But he who has blemished other men by his own selfish ways will not set foot in the House of the Lord.
1.16 For God looks upon all men as His creation.
1.17 Whomever shall defile what God has created, shall himself be cast into eternal damnation.
1.18 And do not look to Me to right what My Father has determined to be a wrong.
1.19 Look instead into your own hearts and souls for My Father has given you the knowledge to understand when there is hatred in your eyes and defilement in your own hands.

The Fictional Book of Jesus

Chapter 3

1.1 Moses and Elijah will one day stand astride the Son of God, not in His Father's Kingdom but here on Earth.
1.2 For the Lord's prophets do the Father's bidding.
1.3 They keep and protect His Son from all harm until the day that is to come.
1.4 I await that day not with joy but with the knowing that it is to be what must be.
1.5 Liken it unto a farmer who tends his fields.
1.6 In the spring, he tills the land turning up the ground for a new rebirth.
1.7 So too does the Father turn men's souls to the way and the light.
1.8 Then the farmer plants his seedlings and with much hope, he nourishes and nurtures them.
1.9 So too does the Father who sent his only begotten Son to plant the seed of Faith on this Earth.
1.10 With words and deeds, he nourishes men's souls to prepare them for their rebirth.
1.11 During the growing season, the farmer watches his plants flourish and his fruit blossom.
1.12 So does the Father who lends strength and comfort to His Son to prepare Him for what is to come.
1.13 When the harvest is in, the farmer rejoices in his crops and brings them to market where he proudly shows them to all who would be interested.
1.14 So too does the Father. He exults in the souls who have come over to His cause and rejected evil.
1.15 Pleased with his faithful congregation, He lavishes praise upon them and provides them with everlasting comfort.
1.16 Therefore, shall it be that this day forward, anyone who rejects the many evils and abominations of the world and walks in My footsteps, shall experience the eternal salvation of My Father.

The Fictional Book of Jesus

Chapter 4

1.1 It will come to pass that I will spread the Word of My Father to the ends of the Earth.

1.2 I will gather disciples one by one to explain to all of humanity what My Father expects of His people.

1.3 These disciples will follow their Lord not due to an obligation or an order from their Pharisee but because they heard the Word of God from the Son of God and they believed.

1.4 And these disciples, if they so be clean even unto death, shall live for all eternity with Me and I with them.

1.5 For let it be known, that he who seeks the teachings of the Son of God, will be saved if they believe what they hath seen with thine own eyes.

1.6 If a man came upon his brethren in the road, suffering from no man's affliction and passed him by wouldn't he not expect a reward for his lack of pity?

1.7 If another man came upon this one brethren, still suffering in the road and gave him of food and drink, wouldn't he also not expect a reward for this trifle amount of sympathy?

1.8 If a third man takes in this one brethren who suffers for no man's sake, gives him comfort and tends to his suffering, he shall find his reward a hundred-fold when this one brethren can repay him.

1.9 But I say unto you, the reward this man hath received from this one brethren is but a driblet compared to the reward this man will receive in My Father's Kingdom for My Father sees all, remembers all, and rewards all who are fitting of remuneration.

1.10 For I seek not worldly riches, nor earthly kingdoms, nor vast armies to rule.

1.11 My riches will be the souls of men. My Kingdom will be the Heavens above. My armies will be the believers of My Word.

1.12 My Word will be the Truth and all who follow My teachings shall be saved.

1.13 For let it be known that I have been told this by My Father, your Creator.

Forever Without End

Of all the events that occurred in our lives do we sometimes look back with regret and wish they had happened differently?

It was 1971 and Patsy Grimaldi was like any other Italian-American kid growing up in the era of flower children. Long hair, tie-dyed clothes, facial hair appearing and disappearing based upon what new musical group appeared on American Bandstand during any particular month. A tad taller than six-feet, the girls in school would tell him that he was cute but to Patsy, he didn't understand what that really meant. All he knew were that the girls would giggle when they told him.

He lived with his parents and sister in a middle-class home in Waterfield, an industrial town in the northeast where gray and orange smoke from countless factories spewed their particle-laden chemicals into the air.

The Grimaldi's house sat on a hill and every morning, Patsy would wake up, gaze from the third-floor parlor window, and watch the sun become obliterated by the haze.

"You'll be late for school Pasquale," his mother warned.

Known to his friends as Patsy, his mother referred to him by his given name. Because she measured success by a person's efforts, Patsy's mother saw her son as a disappointment. Although both his intelligence and potential overshadowed his motivation and accomplishments, he was basically a good kid, a morally correct young man. Drinking, drugs, and sex were as foreign to his being as a golf pro trying to hit a baseball with a tennis racquet.

Patsy always had fun and success on the sandlots, but achievements eluded him on the organized teams at high school. Not from a lack of desire but from his point of view, endless sessions of practice made no sense at all. What fun was practice? Playing the game was all that mattered to Patsy, but those worries were long gone. Patsy had graduated high school two years ago.

"I said, you'll be late for school," she warned him again.

Patsy's gaze left the window. "Mom, my first class is at

ten. I won't be late."

"Young man, you still have to shower and dress. Did you finish studying last night?" she asked.

Patsy faced his mom and sized-up the middle-aged woman. His aunts and uncles said his mom was pretty but to a twenty-one-year-old, anyone in their fifties was past pretty. She ran the household with an iron fist and always reminded Patsy that he was a problem.

He wasn't like his sister, Philomena. She was earning straight-A's in high school. The failing grades he had received in high school were made up in summer school. The IQ tests didn't lie. His teachers and even the principal had commented to Mrs. Grimaldi that Pasquale was borderline genius. He just needed to apply himself. But then again, IQ tests weren't like high school football practice to Patsy. To him, the IQ tests were game day and the league championship was on the line. He didn't have to study for them.

"Well, what are you waiting for?" Patsy's mom now walked up to him and demanded action. "Go get ready, now." Her screams were followed by the distinct sound of tapping beneath the linoleum covered floor coming from the second-floor tenants. "See what you've done! Now the Salentinos know what a cattivo ragazzo you are."

"Mom, I'm not a boy. I'm in college."

"College, you call that two-year school college? You flunked so many times in high school and had to get Bs in summer school just so you could play on the football team. That two-year school was the only college that would accept you because they wanted your father's hard-earned money more than they wanted you."

Patsy grabbed the clothes from his bedroom and ran to the bathroom. He shut the door and from inside he pleaded, "I'm trying, mom. I'll do better."

"You better do better," she screamed. "All you care about is sports and dinosaurs. They won't put food on the table or buy you a house. Smart girls are looking for doctors and lawyers to marry. Do you want to end up like your father, working in a dirty factory the rest of your life?"

Patsy stared in the mirror as a tear rolled down his cheek. I wish someone really cared about me, he thought to himself.

Pounding on the door accompanied a shout, "Hurry up, your sister has to finish in there. Don't make her late for the bus."

Patsy quickly showered and dressed. He walked outside the bathroom as Philomena pushed her way past him.

Patsy grabbed his books and left the apartment. He ran down the winding stairway to the ground floor. Mister Testa, the owner of the three-family house was having a cup of coffee on the back porch. It was early June and he was admiring the tomato vines he had just planted. Patsy spotted him and said, "Hi Mister Testa."

With a spattering of broken English, Mister Testa answered, "Pasquale, why you no cuta you hair?"

Breaking stride for just seconds, and facing Mister Testa as he walked backwards, Patsy replied, "All the kids are wearing it like this now."

"You not all a kids, you a good-da boy."

"Haven't you heard of the Beatles? Their *Let It Be* album came out last year. Did you see the cover, they wear their hair long and even started growing beards and mustaches," remarked Patsy as he used his hand to brush back his curly black hair.

"You wanta look brutto?" replied the elderly man.

"No, I just want to fit in," replied Patsy who then ran down the porch steps toward his car.

Mister Testa waved his hand. "Ah, lei è brutto."

Patsy unlocked the driver's door of his 1964 maroon Chevy Impala and tossed his books on the back seat. He revved the engine and drove away from the house, across town to the Mattabesic Community College campus.

Tucked in the western hills of the city, it was a sprawling array of temporary trailers and park benches. The one community building that served as a cafeteria was a gathering place for students. Patsy parked his car and walked up to the building. His friend Michael Rizza was waiting for him sitting on a bench along the sidewalk that meandered through the campus.

"Hey, amico, did you study for today's final exam?" Michael asked while he took a swig from a bottle of Coca Cola.

"Yeah, I studied," replied Patsy as he took a seat on the bench next to his friend.

Michael asked "So, what are your plans after graduation?"

"I'm playing my last summer of Legion ball," Patsy

boasted.

"No, I mean work. You got a real job? And I don't mean that grocery story gig." Michael asked and took another sip.

Patsy smiled. "I applied to Yale."

Michael coughed as Coca Cola spurted from his nose. "You what?"

"You heard me."

"Why?"

"Why not?"

Michael laughed. "Hey man, even if you could afford to go there, there's no way you'd get accepted anyway."

"I know my high school grades weren't good, but I've gotten nothing but all As and a few Bs ever since I've enrolled in community college."

Michael scoffed, "Hey man, you're just living a pipe dream."

"I got the money."

"What?"

"I've got the money to go to Yale."

"Are you kidding me?"

"No."

"Where'd your parents get the cash?"

"Not my parents."

Michael laughed. "You got some hidden source of funds?"

"My Nonna."

"You're grandmother? But she's dead."

"She left me money. It's in a secret place. Even my parents don't know about the money."

"How's that?"

"I can't tell you."

"So how much?"

"Enough to pay for two years at Yale."

"Man, you're full of surprises."

Patsy held Michael's arm. "Don't pass on to anyone what I just told you."

"I won't."

"Promise?"

Michael pulled his arm away. "Yes, I promise."

The boys leaned back and watched the other students pass by. Patsy stared at several coeds but the only one who returned his glance gave him a sneer.

Michael jabbed his friend. "Did you see that? She ain't got no respect."

"She doesn't have any respect," corrected Patsy.

Michael responded, "That's what I said, didn't you hear me? Get that manicotti out of your ears." Then Michael changed the subject. "She's dating that redhead Irish guy. What's his name, Bobby O'Dwyer I think?"

"O'Brien."

"What?"

"O'Brien is his name," corrected Patsy.

"O'Dwyer, O'Brien, it doesn't matter. He's Irish, right?"

"Yeah."

"So, you still dating that Laura Wilson girl?" Michael asked.

Patsy turned to his friend and stared. "Why? If I say no, are you going to ask her out?"

"Maybe, why?"

"Good luck."

"Why do you say that?"

"It's just that we get into an argument every time we're out on a date. We decided to take a timeout."

"That's because she wants it."

"Yeah, right."

"You got to give her what she wants," Michael laughed and nudged Patsy. "Her old boyfriend said she's easy."

"I'm still looking."

Michael half-smiled and whispered, "Are you still a virgin?"

"I told you, I'm still looking."

Michael laughed. "So that's it. And that's why you're not dating Laura?"

"I'm going to tell her it's over between us," Patsy said facing Michael.

"Here's your chance, she's coming now."

Patsy turned his head and his face flushed red. He felt a flutter inside his chest. Laura walked toward him as Patsy tried to regain his composure.

"Hi Laura."

"Hi," she said as she slowed to talk to Patsy. "What's going on?" she asked.

"Patsy has something to tell you," Michael replied.

"What do you want to tell me?" Laura asked.

"I'll tell you later," Patsy replied.

"Tell me now. I have to meet someone in ten minutes."

"Yeah, tell her now," prodded Michael who flashed an ear-to-ear grin.

Patsy felt the warmth envelop his whole body as he searched for the courage to confront Laura.

"Well?" Laura asked.

"We're...I mean...I'm not going to see you anymore," Patsy blurted.

"Is that all?" Laura asked.

"Yeah, I guess so."

"All right then. I guess I'm free on Saturday, right?"

"Yeah."

"Good, Mark Bailey asked me to go with him to the Irish Festival. So, I'm going."

"You're going with him?" Patsy asked.

"Yeah, you're going with him?" Michael asked.

"Yes," Laura replied and with that, she left the two boys in her wake.

"Lucky Mark but wow, she's a real pain. I see what you mean," Michael said.

The horn sounded on campus and everyone hurried to their class. Patsy took the test. Unlike high school where he didn't have a sense of urgency for study, he was comfortable with community college. The desire to do well now resided within him.

Patsy spent the remainder of the day taking two more finals. His semester was now over, and he ran to the community building. On the walls, he hunted for the posted final grades of the courses he had taken exams for earlier in the week. He searched for his subjects, teachers, and classes. He found them and whispered, "All right." One final grade was a B+ and the other an A-.

Patsy drove home with a smile on his face. He parked his car in front of the house and ran up the steps. Patsy opened the door and found his family seated at the dinner table to a meal of ziti and meatballs.

"Where have you been?" asked his mother.

"Two of my grades were a B+ and A-," Patsy boasted and

then sat at the kitchen table.

"Answer your mother," Patsy's father instructed.

"I looked for my posted grades after school."

"B-plus, why not two As?" Patsy's mother asked. His sister laughed and his mother slammed her fork on the table. She looked at her daughter and said, "Shut up or I'll send you to right to bed."

"Connie, she didn't do anything wrong," her husband pleaded.

"Shut up Sal or this will be the last cooked meal you'll get this week. And you," she pointed to Patsy. "Why didn't you pray to your Nonna for good grades? She would have answered your prayers if you only asked. Have you no faith?"

Patsy rolled his eyes. "Momma, I pray to God all the time and He never answers my prayers."

"God is too busy looking after everyone else. He doesn't know you, Nonna knows you, and she loved you ever since you were a little baby. I wiped her tears when she held you in her arms at the hospital. Now she's an angel in Heaven waiting for you to pray to her."

"Connie, that reminds me. Have you found the key to Nonna's trunk that's still in our basement cage?"

"No, why don't you just pry it open?"

"Oh no, that trunk's been in our family for generations, since before they arrived from Naples. A crowbar would damage it forever." Sal turned to Patsy. "Have you seen the key to Nonna's trunk?"

"Have I what?" Patsy asked.

"Have you seen the key to Nonna's trunk?"

Patsy hesitated. "What key?"

"The key to Nonna's trunk," Connie yelled. "Have you seen it?"

Patsy closed his eyes and then said, "Why, do you think I would have it and not tell you about it?"

Sal put his hand on Patsy's arm. "No son, we're not accusing you of having it." He turned to his wife. "Connie, we can look for the key to the trunk later. Now let's all have supper together and then we'll all sit in the parlor and watch television."

The boy stared at the food on his table and said, "I'm going to skip dinner. I can't play hoops with that in my stomach."

"If you don't eat with us, you're not going anywhere," his mother replied.

Patsy sat at the table and explained, "But if I don't get to the park soon, the guys will have already decided on teams. I won't get to play."

"Never mind basketball, you eat with us," his mother demanded. As Patsy reluctantly spooned ziti in his dish, she asked, "Are you working at the store tonight?"

"I start working the dayshift next week," Patsy replied.

"Can you stop there tonight and bring home eggplant?" his father asked.

"Yeah, I can."

"Tomorrow we'll have eggplant parmigiana," his mother said.

After a few minutes of silence, Patsy spoke up and asked, "Why can't I go to the park and play some basketball with the guys?"

Patsy's mother said, "No, I don't like the boys who hang around there. They look like a bunch of hoodlums."

"Sure, you can go." Sal said. He looked at Connie and winked his eye. "After taking those exams and before you start work next week, you need a break. Finish your meal and then you can go."

Patsy's mother at first didn't say a word and then relented, "All right. Be home before it gets dark."

"I promise I will," Patsy replied.

Patsy finished dinner and helped clear the table. He pulled on a pair of cut-off blue jeans and an oversized tee shirt, red with the gold letters SAINT MICHAEL THE ARCHANGEL written across the front. He grabbed the basketball from his room, said goodbye to his parents and his sister and ran down the stairs to his car.

It was a short drive to the park. Certainly, it was within walking distance, but it was a status symbol to drive there. Patsy thought, perhaps one of the neighborhood girls would want to go to that new McDonalds restaurant near where the Interstate highway ends. It was a good parking spot, dark, and away from home. It was safe from the trouble that always erupted near the downtown shopping plaza.

Patsy parked his car on the outside of the fence that

wound its way about the perimeter of the park. He got out of his car, grabbed his basketball, and noticed the guys playing three-on-three on the court.

To Patsy, it was always important to scout the people on the court. He could tell how long of a wait it would be before he could play, based upon the teams likely to be eliminated. He sized up the other guys hanging around and projected the team he'd likely be on. He dribbled his basketball and walked up to his friend Bill.

"Are you on a team yet?"

"Yeah, me, Joe, and Mike are all set."

"Who's not on a team?" Patsy asked.

Bill pointed to two younger kids standing on the sidelines. "Dave and Chuck."

"They're high school kids," Pasty said.

"I know but that's all that's left."

Patsy asked, "How long of a wait? Maybe someone will leave on the other teams and I can fill in."

Bill said, "I doubt it. It's about an hour wait. Two teams are ahead of me and the loser of this game plays the winner of the next game."

Patsy looked at his watch and saw that it was already after seven. An hour wait would put any game's end close to darkness and he remembered what his mother said.

"Hey, I'm going to pass on a game tonight. I might run to McDonalds. Want to skip your game and come with me?"

"No way, I'll stay here," Bill replied.

Patsy nodded and left the park. On his way out, he saw two girls and recognized them as high school seniors. He asked one of them, Sara, if she wanted to go to McDonalds with him.

"Drop dead!" she exclaimed as her friend laughed.

Patsy touched the one acne blemish on his cheek, tossed the ball on the backseat in his car, and drove off. He got onto the Interstate and headed toward the end of the highway. Once past the amber flashing lights and the red and white wooden barriers on the exit ramp, he pulled into the McDonalds parking lot. He drove his car around to the back and shut the engine.

A familiar shiny blue late model Camaro rested under the trees. It belonged to John Miles, the renowned sophomore quarterback at Syracuse who was on Patsy's old high school football team. He was a three-sport athlete at Saint Michael the Archangel and was trying to duplicate that trifecta in the car with three women. One of them could have been his girlfriend Sue, or maybe one was Valerie, or Donna, though he would probably boast that it was all three.

Patsy shook his head and remembered the last game of his senior year against cross-town rival Roosevelt High. Patsy was the team's main kick returner and finally got into the offensive lineup when his team wasn't ahead or behind by three touchdowns. The score was 22-16 with Saint Michael the Archangel ahead and with control of the ball.

They were playing a split-T formation, 3rd and five to go on their own 16-yard line in the 4th quarter with 2:45 left to play. Coach Sorrento sent in a play, power pitch right. It was a play meant to open a lane down the right sideline. Designed to provide the fullback with a chance to break a long run, the quarterback, halfback, tight end, and pulling right guard would provide the blocking. Patsy would carry the ball and he was ready, boy was he ready. Those long, boring days of practice would finally pay off.

John Miles was under center and Patsy was drooling in the backfield. But there were college scouts in the stands that day. Rumor had it that they were from Syracuse, exactly where Miles planned to go.

When the center hiked the ball, everything seemed to move in slow motion for Patsy. He ran to the right expecting a pitch from Miles, but the quarterback never released the ball, instead he kept it. Patsy stopped and stood in the backfield and watched Miles run through a hole that the team bus could have driven through. Eighty-four yards for a touchdown and just like that, the game was out of reach for Roosevelt. Mobbed by the rest of the team, Miles smiled when he saw Patsy and then mockingly laughed at him. His team went on to win 30-16 and Miles got his full scholarship to Syracuse.

Patsy waited in the car for twenty minutes, though it seemed longer to him. A few couples made out in the dark part of the lot and some kids hung around near the front door. Out of the corner of his eye, Patsy saw a blue blur arrive in his field of vision. It was Officer McKenna.

"Hey there, you Guinea-dago-wop, what are you doing?

Oh, you're the Grimaldi boy, aren't you?" Officer McKenna asked.

"Yes sir," Patsy replied.

"Did you make a purchase?"

"What?"

"Did you buy anything inside?" Officer McKenna pointed toward the restaurant with his nightstick.

"No sir," Patsy answered.

"Then get a move on or your old man will be picking you up at the station."

Patsy again looked at the blue Camaro and then said something he should have reconsidered, "Why do you allow John Miles to park over there?"

The officer looked over his shoulder at the parked car under the trees where young girls' laughter seemed to emanate. "Because Johnny Miles was just nominated by "The Sporting News" as their preseason, First-team All-American Quarterback," Officer McKenna replied.

"First-team? He's a sophomore at Syracuse."

The policeman grinned and replied, "As a sophomore he threw for almost three-thousand yards, tossed twenty-two touchdowns, and ran for more than a thousand yards. Now, more is expected of our town's biggest hero in his junior year. Hey, maybe someday he'll play for the New York Giants." Then Officer McKenna's smile evaporated. "Now get the hell out of here, Grimaldi."

Patsy started his car and left the parking lot. He watched Officer McKenna twirling his nightstick in his rear-view mirror as he drove away.

Back on the Interstate, Patsy flicked on the radio and after a few short comments from the DJ, the hauntingly beautiful Simon & Garfunkel song, Bridge Over Troubled Water began.

Patsy listened to the tune and took the words to heart. Tears dripped from his eyes as the song wove its message throughout his thoughts. He longed for someone to give him purpose in life, someone that would bring everything into focus for him.

"Oh Nonna, please send me someone to love."

Patsy decided to stop at the local Rite-Aid pharmacy and drove into the parking lot, stopping next to a dark green Pontiac. He walked into the store and made a bee line for aisle seven and the acne cream. He reviewed the varieties before selecting one he'd tried before.

Just as he was leaving for the register, he heard a giggle from the next aisle. Patsy walked to the front of the store and reached the end of the aisle. A blond girl, a girl that he had never seen in town cut in front of him from the next aisle. Patsy got in line behind the girl and patiently waited while the sales person served the other customers.

He got a good view of the back of the young girl. He noticed that her blond hair ran below her shoulders as he snuck glimpses of her shape. All were pleasing to his eyes as he spied her every movement. When she was next in line, another cashier opened a second register and announced, "I can take whose next."

Patsy instinctively took one step forward as the girl made a move toward the second register. They bumped slightly. "I'm sorry, go ahead," Patsy said.

"Are you sure?" the girl asked.

"Yes, of course. Go ahead."

"That's sweet," she said.

Sweet? That's sweet she said, he thought. Patsy waited and when she was done at the register, she walked away and met a girl with short brown hair waiting at the front door. They left while Patsy stared and watched them disappear into the parking lot as the cashier said to him, "I don't have all night!"

He paid for his acne cream and left the store. As Patsy walked to his car, he saw the green Pontiac pull out of the lot and drive away. He climbed into his car and drove off.

He hadn't driven more than two miles when he saw a green Pontiac parked in a gas station with its hood up. Two girls, a blonde, and a brunette stood next to the car along with the garage mechanic.

Patsy watched the girls as he drove by and the blonde looked up and made eye contact with him. That's the girl from the drugstore, Patsy thought. He signaled left, pulled onto a side street, and doubled back. He drove into the gas station and parked behind the Pontiac.

"Do you have car trouble?" he asked as he stuck his head through the open driver's window.

The blonde looked up while the brunette said, "There's

that guy from the drugstore."

"Can I give you a lift?" Patsy asked.

Before the girls could speak, the mechanic said, "Car's OK. You just had a loose sparkplug wire. It was misfiring." The mechanic closed the hood.

"No that's OK," the brunette replied to Patsy's offer. "We don't need a ride."

"Well how about if I follow you home just to make sure you don't get stuck again?" Patsy asked.

"All right," replied the blonde as she smiled at Patsy.

The brunette rolled her eyes and climbed into the driver's side. The blonde got in and they left with Patsy following close behind. It was a short drive to an apartment complex where the girls and Patsy parked their cars. The brunette opened one of the apartment doors and walked inside. Just as the blonde was about to do the same, Patsy asked her, "Can I speak with you?"

She stopped and looked at Patsy. "Sure, I'll be right out."

Patsy sat on the steps and waited. After about ten minutes, she came out and sat next to Patsy.

"Hi, my name's Patsy," he said and held out his hand.

The girl took his hand and replied, "Well Patsy, I'm Inga Keller and my friend's name is Judy. What's your last name?"

"Grimaldi."

"Patrick Grimaldi?"

"No, it's not Patrick. It's Patsy, short for Pasquale."

"Pasquale Grimaldi? Wow, now that's a real cool name."

"Do you think so?"

Inga nodded and said with a Midwestern accent, "Oh yah."

Patsy asked, "Do you live here?"

"No, we're just visiting Judy's older sister and her husband. We're from Grand Rapids, Michigan."

"How long will you be here?" Patsy asked.

"About a week." Inga laughed. "But it's going to seem like forever."

"My father has an expression. Forever without end."

"What does that mean?" Inga asked.

"A lot of people say they'll stay with someone forever, but my dad always says he'll stay with my mom forever without end."

"That's sweet."

The door to the apartment opened and Judy stuck her

head out. "Inga, my sister needs our help. Come on inside."

When Judy closed the door, Inga stood up and said, "I have to go."

Patsy got up but before Inga went inside, he asked, "Can I see you again?"

Inga turned around. "We're going to the beach tomorrow but I'm not doing anything at night."

"Can I call you?" Patsy asked.

"Just a minute," Inga disappeared into the apartment.

Patsy closed his eyes and saw Inga's face imprinted in his thoughts. She reminded him of one of the participants he saw in the last Miss America Beauty Pageant; the innocent face, the sculpted body, the long golden, silky hair. When Patsy heard the screen door open, he became startled and awakened from his reverie. He watched Inga hand over a slip of paper. "What's this?" he asked.

"It's the phone number here. Call me about six tomorrow night. I'll be in."

"All right, I'll call you then."

"OK, good night."

"Good night."

Patsy turned toward his car and looked back a few times. Each time he glanced at her, Inga was still looking at him, still smiling. Was this too good to be true? He got in his car and drove off.

As he headed toward the grocery store to buy eggplant, a smile grew on his face and he turned on the radio. The Carpenters' song 'Close to You' was playing and Patsy tried to sing along. He couldn't wait for tomorrow night to arrive.

The next day was spent in anticipation of Patsy's evening phone call to Inga. When six o'clock arrived, he called and she told him that she was tired, but he could always drop by and they would listen to music together. Patsy was overjoyed.

A quick explanation to his parents that he was going to visit a friend was met with skepticism from his mother, but his father vouched for him and Patsy was home free.

When he arrived at the apartment, Inga dressed in hip-hugger bell-bottom jeans and a white midriff top, greeted him at the door. Patsy soon learned that Judy was at a neighborhood party with her sister and brother-in-law.

Inga invited Patsy into the living room, and she put Led Zeppelin's first record album on the stereo. As the opening track, *Good Times Bad Times* played Patsy asked Inga all about herself. She explained that after graduating high school she had hitchhiked to Connecticut with her friend from Michigan. Her admission of having tried nearly every recreational drug shocked Patsy but by then he was mesmerized by her face, her hair, and her body. At that point she could have confessed that she was a serial killer and pulled out a rope, knife, and poison and Patsy would have simply nodded with awestruck eyes.

Patsy reached out with his right hand and touched the back of her right hand. To his surprise she didn't push it away but instead turned her hand over. Her fingers searched for his as their eyes met. Patsy felt her fingers intertwine with his and then grasp his hand. The rhythmic tapping from the tips of her fingers against the back of his hand and the stroking of her thumb against the inside base of his wrist caused a flutter inside his chest.

Inga laid her head down on the back of the couch, turned and stared at Patsy. He did the same, facing Inga. When he noticed her eyes close and her head move closer to him, he reached out and clasped his hand on the side of her waist.

Patsy felt Inga's arm caress the back of his shoulder. It prompted him to get closer to her and their lips met.

At first, the kiss was simply a gesture of affection for one another. As the evening progressed and their conversation slowly dwindled, they began French-kissing.

The front door opened at ten and Judy, a bit inebriated, laughed and went upstairs to bed. Nearly a half-hour later, the couple in residence returned, introduced themselves, and then also went upstairs.

By midnight, when Patsy began to explore and massage the bare skin between Inga's midriff top and hip-hugger bell bottom jeans, Inga told Patsy that it was time for him to go.

"Can I see you again tomorrow?"

"Yes, just drop by the same time."

"All right."

Pasty received a goodnight kiss at the door.

Then Inga said, "Hey Patsy, forever without end."

Inga smiled and Patsy returned one in kind.

Another day spent in anticipation of another evening with

Inga left Patsy wishing the time would fly by. When it was nearly six p.m. he left for the apartment. When he got there, he rang the bell, the door opened, and Judy's sister appeared.

"They're not here."

"What do you mean? Inga said to stop by," Patsy said.

Judy's sister said, "All I know is they said they were going out."

"When they come back please tell her to call me," Patsy said handing Judy's sister a piece of paper with his phone number written on it.

Patsy had driven a couple of miles from the apartment when he spotted a green Pontiac headed toward him. He recognized Inga in the passenger seat and her friend was driving. Patsy turned his car around and followed them.

It appeared to Patsy that the driver knew she was being followed because it sped up and turned down a side road in an apparent attempt to elude Patsy's car. Nevertheless, he followed and pushed his car to the limit

Bare-knuckle driving, squealing tires, burnt rubber, up to fifty miles an hour on residential roads but the Pontiac would not slow down. Patsy's eyes moistened as he thought of Inga inside the car and how these actions were a mystery to him. When the Pontiac pulled into a driveway to turn around, Patsy parked his Chevy and blocked the car.

Judy got out and yelled, "Move your car!"

Pasty poked his head out the driver's window. "Let me see Inga."

"Move your damn car!"

"Not until I see Inga." Patsy got out of his car and walked up to Judy.

"She never wants to see you again. How'd you like my driving?"

"What?" Pasty stared at Judy confused at the sudden shift in her mood.

"You barely kept up with me," Judy said as she laughed.

Patsy shook his head. "Yeah, right. Let me see Inga."

"She's in the front seat but I doubt she'll be able to talk to you."

Patsy walked over to the passenger door and looked inside. The sight he saw made him shudder. Inga was seated with her head hung low. When he tapped on the window Inga looked up. Her golden hair was tossed in disarray and laced drool dangled from her mouth suspended onto her shirt and arms. Patsy stared at her glassy eyes with their five-hundred-mile gaze.

"Inga!" Patsy turned to Judy and with both concern and hatred in his voice demanded, "What did you do to her?"

"We went to that shopping plaza at the end of the highway."

"You what?"

"We met this guy there named John Miles and he sold us some horse."

"Horse?"

"We snorted heroin."

"Drugs, why?"

"Why not?"

Patsy and Judy both looked up when they heard a screen door open.

"Get the hell out of my yard before I call the police!" A woman screamed as she ran down her front steps.

Patsy reassured the homeowner. "Don't worry lady I was just trying to help the girl in the car."

The woman's tone mellowed, and she asked, "Is everything all right? Does someone need a doctor?"

"No, everything is all right. We're leaving now," Judy said.

"Do you want me to follow you home?" Patsy asked.

Judy shook her head. "No, let me take care of her. She just needs to sleep it off."

Pasty got in his car and turned around. He followed the Pontiac until they reached a stop sign. A left turn would be in the direction of the apartment and a right turn would be in the direction of Patsy's home.

The Pontiac turned left and after a long moment and with tears in his eyes, Patsy turned right.

The next day, he showed up at the apartment late in the afternoon. A knock on the front door summoned Judy's sister.

"Yes?"

"Hi, I'm the guy who was here last night looking for Inga. Can I see her?"

"She's not here."

"Where is she?"

"She left with my sister this morning."

"Where?"

"They went to Cape Cod."

"But I need to see her. When will they be back?"

"They won't be back."

"What? Can you give me her address back home?"

"I don't know it."

"Then give me Judy's address. I'll send her a letter for Inga."

"I'm not giving my sister's address to a stranger."

"I'm not a stranger."

"You are to me," Judy's sister replied and slammed the door in Patsy's face.

The following day while at work in the produce department at the local Stop & Shop, Patsy asked his boss, "Sally, can you help me?"

Salvatore DeMartino was the assistant produce manager and a transplanted Brooklynite and former longshoreman. An unmarried, 44-year old, he left that demanding job with the intent to ease into retirement in the less hectic lifestyle of Connecticut. Sally's former life was spent in the rough and tumble area that comprised the neighborhoods along Fulton Street, Rockaway Avenue, and Atlantic Avenue. There, you were either a member of the mob or you made sure that you looked the other way.

Sally stared at Patsy, then lifted the cigar from his lips and placed it down on the counter next to the film wrapping machine.

"What's up, kid," Patsy asked.

"I met this girl from Grand Rapids Michigan. I think I'm falling in love with her."

"What's her name?"

"Inga."

"Ingrid, huh. Swedish?"

"I don't think so. Her last name is Keller."

"Oh, Ingrid Keller. Sounds German."

"Yeah, I guess. I had a date with her, but she stood me up. I think her friend convinced her to do some drugs."

Patsy watched Sally crane his neck about the produce backroom. Then Sally said, "Let's go in the cooler."

They threw on their jackets and stepped inside the refrigerated cooler.

"Take a seat but watch out for black widows in those crates of Victoria Reds. The spiders like to hide inside the grape bunches," Sally said.

They settled inside the cooler and Patsy said, "She's blond and beautiful."

"Hey kid, so was Marilyn Monroe but so are a million other women. Forget about her."

"I can't."

"Why not?"

"There's something about her. I feel like we've got this special connection. I'm also sensing that she's vulnerable and has a sadness about her."

"Vulnerable, how?"

"Like she's easily manipulated."

"You can't save her."

"Why not?"

"Because you don't have to. There's plenty of fish in the sea."

"Sally, every life is important. If we ignore the most vulnerable of us, then what have we gained?" Patsy felt the heat from Sally's penetrating stare.

Then Sally said, "If you want me to take a road trip with you to Michigan, I'll go."

A tear streaked down Patsy's cheek. "That's very kind and generous of your time but my parents would never allow it, and I don't even know Inga's address."

"It won't be difficult to locate her once we're in Grand Rapids."

Patsy was silent for a long moment. Then he stood. "I had my chance the other night. I could have followed them back to the apartment and showed my concern for Inga. I didn't and went home." He wiped a tear off his cheek. "Oh, the hell with it. I'll just go on with my life as it was before I met her."

#

On a rainy day in early August, Patsy with hope and expectation in his heart and a portfolio under his arm, walked into the Department of Geology & Geophysics office building on the Yale University campus in New Haven Connecticut. As soon as he entered the doorway, he closed his umbrella.

When he reached the department office, he addressed the receptionist, "I'm a transfer student, and I have a 10 a.m. meeting interview with the Director of Undergraduate Studies."

The receptionist glanced down at a list of names and then said, "Mister Pasquale Grimaldi?"

"Yes."

"Oh, I'm so sorry. Director Kelly had to cancel all his appointments today. Early this morning, the department chair scheduled an unplanned staff meeting that will last until 3 p.m."

"No one told me that my interview was cancelled," Patsy said.

"We called everyone between 8:00 and 8:30 this morning and told them of the cancellation."

"I live in Waterfield and to get here on time, I had to leave home at 7:30." Patsy lifted his sleeve and noted the time on his wristwatch, nine-forty-five. "When can I reschedule?"

The receptionist tapped her pen on the desk and thumbed through her appointment book. "Let's see, how about 1 p.m. next Friday?"

"No that's not good. Starting next week, I'm training a new employee who's replacing me once I start school. This week is the only time I have."

"Director Kelly is busy the rest of this week."

Patsy shook his head. "I was hoping to see him today."

The receptionist glanced at the director's daily schedule. "I'll tell you what. Is that your application under your arm?"

Patsy looked down. "My portfolio? I have other supporting documents as well."

"Leave them with me. Can you return around four this afternoon? Director Kelly has another meeting tonight at seven and he's planning to have dinner in his office. I'm sure I can convince him to review your portfolio and then meet with you between four and six."

"I can do that."

Patsy turned to walk away when the receptionist said, "Are you staying on campus?"

Patsy stopped and looked back. "I have nowhere else to go."

"I have an idea. Why not visit the Peabody Museum and

perhaps even our library?"

Patsy said, "I visit the museum every year and I've been to the library. I've got sneakers in my car. Maybe I'll just go for a jog."

"You can't do that. It's raining outside." The receptionist took a deep breath and then opened her desk drawer. "I've got an idea. Here's a guest pass to the fieldhouse. They have an indoor running track and this pass will get you inside and entitle you to a pair of shorts, a shirt, socks, and a towel."

Patsy took the day pass. "Thank you. I'll do that."

He drove to the Coxe Cage fieldhouse, went down to the locker rooms, showed his pass to the attendant and received a pair of shorts, socks, a shirt and a towel. When Patsy made it upstairs to the running track, he stared in awe of the immenseness of the facility. At the other end of the building, opposite the massive viewing stand was a banner that nearly stretched the width of the structure. It read, <u>YALE BULLDOGS</u>.

A few other people milled in the building. There were three athletes running on the elliptical red track with its running lanes marked in white. One person, presumably a coach with a whistle hanging from a lanyard around his neck, was having a meeting off to the side of the building with seven other athletes. Finally, a man dressed in a sport jacket was leading a boy with broad shoulders and his parents in a tour of the facility.

Patsy kept an eye on all the people making sure that he did not interfere with any of their activities. After he made three laps of the track, he noticed the man in the sports jacket walking toward him. The boy and his parents that the man was speaking to were headed away toward the door.

"Young fella, can I speak with you?" the man in the sports jacket asked.

Patsy stopped jogging and then turned to face the man. "I have a pass, sir."

"What? No, I'm not looking to check your student pass. I want to ask you a question," the man said.

Patsy took a few deep breaths and then rested his hands on his hips. "Yes sir, what is it?"

"Do you know who Carm Cozza is?"

"Yes, of course. He's a legend here."

"Well, I'm his running backs coach. Did you ever consider

going out for the football team?"

"You mean the Yale football team?"

"Yes, you are a student here, aren't you?"

"Well sir, you see I'm not a student yet."

"Why not?"

"I'm in the process of registering."

"I think I know you. Didn't we scout you in high school?"

"I don't think so."

"What's your name, son?"

"Pasquale Grimaldi."

"You play college ball elsewhere?"

"I went two years to Mattabesic Community College."

"JUCO transfer?"

"Oh, no sir. They don't have a football team."

"Good that gives you a possible four years of eligibility. I'll have to double-check the NCAA rules. Where did you play high school football?"

"Saint Michael the Archangel."

"In Waterfield?"

"Yes."

"I knew it. Carm sent me and my assistant there once to scout a player. We lost him to Syracuse. The name was John Miles. You know him?"

"Yeah, he was our quarterback."

"Well, it's a good thing that we didn't recruit him."

"Why?" Patsy asked.

"Didn't you hear? He just got arrested last night."

"What for?"

"Selling dope out of his car in a shopping plaza off the interstate. He's bound to lose his scholarship." The man then turned his attention back to Patsy. "What position did you play, son?"

"Fullback."

"What was your number?"

"Thirty-seven."

"Oh yes, now I remember you. I was very impressed with your athletic ability. Didn't you run back punts and kickoffs?"

"Yeah, I did."

"I watched you return a kickoff for a touchdown against Saugatuck High. How many TDs did you score running back punts and kicks?"

"One my sophomore year, two my junior year, and five my senior year."

"Impressive."

"Yeah, well I wish I played more. It was so difficult getting on the field for snaps."

"I don't know why you didn't. You had the speed and the moves, and you've got a grown man's body. Just look at your calves," the man said.

"Coach Sullivan didn't like me. At least that's what some of my teammates told me."

"You know, in that game we scouted, your team was losing in the 4th quarter and I recall telling my assistant, 'they oughta put in that kid who ran back that kickoff'. You remember how many yards that went for?"

"I think 87 yards."

"You've got a great memory kid; it went for exactly 88 yards. I'll tell you what; you get yourself registered then come and see me later today. If you're interested, we may have a spot for you on the team."

"Are you serious?"

"I am. We can still add you to the roster. How old are you?"

"Nineteen. I'll be twenty in December."

"What have you been doing since high school to keep yourself in playing shape?"

"I was a three-sport athlete at Mattabesic, cross-country, basketball, and baseball plus the last five summers I played American Legion Baseball."

"Kid, give up the basketball. It'll cripple you for life. You're around six-feet. What do you weigh?"

"Just under two-hundred."

"We'll get you up to 210 by the first game, diet, weight room…the whole nine yards. Our main kick returner blew out his knee last week and all we're left with is some pimply-faced, scrawny kid from Long Island who never played high school varsity football. His dad was a 4-year starter for Yale back in the 40s, so we were pressed to offer him a scholarship."

"I can't imagine what you're saying," Patsy said.

"Believe it."

Patsy smiled. "I'm so grateful. I'll do my best."

The man smiled. "That's the type of attitude we want. You make our team and I'll see to it that Carm considers giving you at least a two-year scholarship. If you think you might want to play baseball too, we'll talk to the baseball coach and see if he can kick it up another year."

"Really?"

"It doesn't happen very often that we have two-sport athletes in college, but I'm impressed with what you did in high school and your obvious physical abilities."

The man offered his hand and Patsy shook it. "What's your name sir?"

"Angelo Fede."

"Did you say, Angelo Fede?" Patsy asked as he felt time standstill.

"Why, is something wrong?"

Patsy said, "Angelo is Italian for Angel and Fede is Italian for faith."

"Oh yeah. My Nonna told my mother to name me Angelo." Mister Fede waved his hand in the air. "She had this thing about angels."

Patsy smiled. "My Nonna is in heaven and she always told me to have faith."

"Yeah, ain't that a coincidence. That's how all Italian grandmothers are."

They parted and after Patsy finished his workout he showered and dressed. He hung around the campus for a while and then at 4 p.m., he headed toward the Department of Geology & Geophysics office building.

The receptionist was still at her desk when Patsy walked inside.

"Hi, I'm back. Is he in?" Patsy asked.

The receptionist looked up. "Yes, Mister Grimaldi. Director Kelly is in and he's ready to see you. Go right in."

Patsy stepped up to the door. The nameplate read:

Peter Kelly, Director
Undergraduate Studies

Patsy knocked.

Of Angels and Miracles: Faith

A voice from inside bellowed, "It's open, come in."

Patsy opened the door and noticed a man who sat behind a desk, his head mired in Patsy's portfolio. "Hello, I'm Pasquale…"

"Yeah right, the Italian kid. Have a seat."

Patsy sat in a chair facing Director Kelly's desk. The silence in the room was deafening while Director Kelly read Patsy's application and transcript.

"Is there anything wrong sir?" Patsy asked.

Director Kelly closed the manila folder, took a deep breath and rested his palm under his chin. "I'm sorry Mister Grimaldi, your application is rejected."

"Why?"

"Your high school grades are poor. You failed at least one subject your freshman and sophomore years."

"But I made those classes up in summer school. I turned those Fs into Bs and As."

"Young man, I hardly place any value at all in summer school makeup classes."

"But I got all As and Bs at Mattabesic Community College."

Director Kelly stood up and pushed his chair aside. "Foolish boy, don't insult my intelligence. You wish to equate community college grades with grades at an Ivy League school?"

"But I scored 1540 on my SATs."

"I think we're done here."

"But I have an IQ score of 147."

"Stupid kid, then you must know by now that you have no chance of getting into Yale."

"Wait, I have the money. I can pay cash."

"Are you trying to bribe me?"

"No, I mean I have the cash to pay my tuition."

Patsy heard commotion outside the office and before he or Director Kelly could speak another word, Coach Fede barged into the office followed by the receptionist.

"What's the meaning of this intrusion?" Director Kelly asked.

With a smile from ear to ear, Coach Fede dropped a document on Director Kelly's desk and said, "Coach Cozza has signed off on a full, two-year football scholarship for this young man."

Everyone shared a gleeful laugh except Director Kelly. "I'm not accepting him into our department's curriculum. He doesn't have the background. Perhaps another department would feel otherwise. Business Management is always looking for warm bodies," Director Kelly said.

"But I want to be a paleontologist," Patsy said.

Director Kelly laughed. "Good luck with that one. You'll never get into my department."

Just then, there was a knock on the door and a man entered the office. "What's going on in here?" the man asked.

"Coach Cozza, sir. Have a seat. What are you doing here?" Director Kelly asked.

"I'm just making sure that my new football recruit doesn't have any issues getting accepted into your department's program." Coach Cozza put his arm around Patsy's shoulders.

Director Kelly stuttered with his words. "Well you see, uh, there's…there's a discrepancy. His high school grades disqualify him from entering Yale."

Coach Cozza removed his arm from Patsy's shoulders and stepped toward Director Kelly. "I heard what was discussed. This boy has a high IQ, a nearly perfect score on his SATs, and his grades have been no lower than a B since high school." Coach Cozza continued, "Peter, remember back in 1965 I pushed for a football scholarship for you when no other Ivy League school would do so." Coach Cozza looked around Director Kelly's office. Now look where you are." Coach Cozza put his hand on Director Kelly's shoulder. "Give the kid a chance. He's overcome a lot of adversity to get where he is today."

Director Kelly cleared his throat. "I'll see what I can do."

Coach Cozza was relentless. "No, I want you to approve his application right now so that he can attend football practice tomorrow." Coach Cozza stepped back to Patsy and again put his arms around Patsy's shoulders. Coach Cozza smiled. "I have faith in this kid."

"Yes coach."

#

That was a long time ago. Now Patsy sat in a room at a

nursing home. In the bed was a woman with long silky white hair.

Entering the room, a nurse asked, "Are you a friend of the family here in Grand Rapids?"

"Well, sort of but I'm not from Michigan. I just arrived," Patsy said. His long hair was now salt & pepper and pulled back into a ponytail.

"Did you vote for Donald Trump yesterday?"

Patsy replied, "I didn't have a chance to vote. I flew in from Connecticut yesterday. A friend of mine told me about her. So, I came to visit as soon as I heard she was here."

The nurse looked at the woman in the bed. "Poor woman. Her husband treated her badly and then died some years ago and I hear her kids never come to see her. In fact, they initiated proceedings and had her deemed incompetent by the court who assigned an involuntary guardianship."

"Will she be all right?" Patsy asked.

The nurse said, "She's catatonic. She had a nervous breakdown from her husband's beatings, his cheating on her, plus the drinking and the drugs she took to cope with the abuse. Then a few months ago she had a stroke. They had to operate and cleared some arterial blockages. The stroke left her with minimal motor function. We have to move her every couple of hours so that she doesn't get bed sores. This all took a toll on her. She's now a ward of the state. The doctors say it's only a matter of weeks. We're going to move her to hospice tomorrow."

"Couldn't she snap out of it?"

"I doubt it."

Patsy pleaded, "What if we could keep her here? I have all the money in the world to pay for her care."

"You'll have to take that up with our business director. Say you look familiar. Do I know you?"

An orderly who had stepped into the room overheard the conversation and said, "Don't you know who that is? He's the scourge of the Detroit Lions."

"Say what?" the nurse said.

The orderly pointed his finger at Patsy. "Tell me if I'm wrong but didn't you sign with the Bears as a twenty-three-year-old undrafted free agent back in 1976 out of Yale?"

"Yeah."

"And didn't you run back a punt for a touchdown against

our Lions?"

Patsy confessed, "Yes."

The orderly pointed to the nurse. "See I told you so."

The nurse waved her hand at the orderly. "That's not what I mean." Then she snapped her fingers. "That's it, Yale. Now I know where I saw you. Weren't you on one of those educational cable channels?"

"I have a series on the National Geographic Channel."

"Yes, aren't you that paleontologist from Yale who digs for dinosaur bones all over the world?"

"Yes," Patsy said.

The nurse laughed. "And you've met with foreign leaders and you have your own yacht, imagine that!"

Patsy corrected her. "It's not a yacht. It's a research vessel and it's owned and funded by the National Geographic Society."

The nurse clapped her hands once. "I knew it. My son watches your show every Saturday morning. What's it called, *Exploring with Pasquale*, right?"

Patsy smiled and nodded. "Yes."

The nurse continued, "He even reads your books. I just bought him a set of your video documentaries." She held her hand out. "Nice to meet you, Mister…"

Patsy spoke before she could finish. "Grimaldi, Pasquale Grimaldi."

"I'll have to tell him that I met you. Maybe I'll bring him by tomorrow if you're still here. Would you autograph your books for him?" the nurse asked.

Patsy said, "I'd be pleased to do so."

The nurse shook Patsy's hand and then left. Patsy glanced at Inga and clutched her hand. It was cold to the touch. He sat on the bed, massaging her hand and whispering to her.

"Inga, where have you been?" He recounted, "Funny, I've been spending most of my adult life digging up dinosaurs that were lost for millions of years. I was searching for the perfect specimen. Although I lost you a long time ago, I've always kept you in my heart."

He continued to massage her hand and whispered, "Oh Nonna, Inga is the only woman I ever cared for and she's been through so much hurt. We've both wandered about for many years but now I've found her again. Please heal her. I would stay by her side for the rest of my life. She needs a blessing and I need a miracle. It would mean so much." Then he turned to Inga and whispered in her ear, "I'll be here for you Inga, forever without end."

With those last words, Patsy felt a slight hand movement. He looked down and Patsy's eye caught a finger move. Then he heard a sound. It was like a rush of air from her lungs and her breath hastened. She exhaled, and her eyes partially opened. She looked at Patsy and he sensed that she immediately recognized him.

"Forever without end," she said weakly squeezing his hand. Then Inga smiled, struggled to push herself up in bed, and grabbed Patsy about his neck.

Patsy felt the strength in her grip and he knew that she was misdiagnosed. "Inga, I'm going to see to it that you get well again."

She hugged him, then kissed him and whispered in his ear, "Where have you been? I've waited for so long."

"I'm here Inga."

Inga pushed herself to the side of the bed and said, "I knew that you would come back to me. I never lost faith."

In My Life

What happens when we die? Are we aware of the life we just lived? Do we meet people we knew on the other side? And finally, is it possible for us to have a second chance to right wrongs that happened in our lives?

"They shot John Lennon."

"What did you say?" Jimmy asked the restaurant manager who had wandered onto the stage and interrupted his acoustic set.

"I said John Lennon got shot."

Jimmy took a step back and sat on his stool. His roaming eyes stared at the tables, chairs, and then at the blank faces of the audience.

"Is he all right?"

The restaurant manager continued barely above a whisper. "Howard Cosell just announced on Monday Night Football that he's dead."

Jimmy glanced at his watch. It was almost midnight. "I can't continue, not now."

The manager placed his hand on Jimmy's shoulder. "Let me announce this, take a break."

Jimmy threw back his long black hair and got up from his stool. Carrying his orange Gretsch 6120 hollow body guitar, he nodded to the patrons and said, "I'll be right back."

After he walked offstage and the manager announced the tragic news to the audience, Jimmy noticed a woman crying. She stood next to a group of people, some covering their mouths with their hands. Near the restrooms, a gaggle of twenty-year-olds rushed into the women's room, their faces swathed in handkerchiefs.

The restaurant owner hurried up to Jimmy. "Did you hear the news?"

Jimmy nodded, stroking his full beard. "What happened?"

"All I know is that some nut shot him in front of Lennon's building in the City. I heard it's called the Dakota." The restaurant owner continued, "What a shame. He seemed like he was a good person. You know, give peace a chance, all you need is love."

Jimmy said, "Yeah, his message was all about treating people right."

"Hey, yesterday you said that you actually met him once."

"I did."

The owner said, "Tell me about it."

Jimmy set his guitar on the cushioned back of a chair in the rear lounge area. "Earlier this year I was heading back to Connecticut and saw him in Penn Station."

"Penn Station, what was he doing there?"

"He was having a sandwich at one of the underground shops. I sat on a stool next to him and we had lunch together."

"Was he alone? I'm surprised he'd be out in public."

Jimmy nodded. "He was alone, in disguise, pulled back hair, sneakers, jeans, a tan overcoat, a fedora, and sunglasses. Oh, I knew it was him. I have all his records. The wall of my room back home is covered with Beatles posters and pictures of him. That disguise didn't fool me, and he knew it."

"But why was he there, and alone?"

"In his own words he said he sometimes liked to get away from the minted knob heads and get all chuffed with the pikeys."

The owner sported a smile. "I don't know what you said but I have an idea. So, what did you two talk about?"

Jimmy pointed to his guitar. "I had just bought this at a friend's store in the City and Lennon asked if he could try it out. We went to a deserted concourse at the station and in a couple of hours he taught me how to play a bunch of his songs." Jimmy shook his head. "I just can't believe he's dead."

The owner was silent for a moment and then asked, "Can you stay a few extra days? I'd like you to play some of his music, and then speak to the audience about your meeting him."

Jimmy hesitated. "I'm not sure. That snowstorm is going to slow me down. I wanted to hop a train back to Connecticut before the weekend, but I have unfinished business here in Syracuse."

"What unfinished business?"

"I was hoping to meet someone."

"Who?"

"A girl."

"Hey, who isn't, any girl in particular?"

"A few years ago, I met a girl in Connecticut. She told me she was from Syracuse. She was gorgeous. She loved the color red. She always made sure she wore something red."

"Red?"

"Yeah, we had a couple of dates and things seemed to be getting serious, but she left before I could say goodbye." Jimmy shook his head, his long straight hair bouncing back and forth. "I swore I wouldn't shave or cut my hair until I saw her again."

"I can help you. I've lived here my whole life. Do you know her address, maybe her name?

"She promised that she'd give me her phone number and address before she left, but she never kept our next date. The girl's name is Heidi Becker."

The owner nodded and then put his head down. "Yeah, I know her, and you're right, she's beautiful. Forget about it, her boyfriend's bad news."

"You have to help me. I never got to tell her how I really feel about her."

"Don't you mean how you really felt about her?"

"No, I still have feelings for her."

The restaurant manager walked up to Jimmy and the owner. "Hey, the audience is ready for you again. They want to hear a John Lennon song. Can you?" he asked.

"Yeah, I guess I can," Jimmy said.

The owner smiled and slapped Jimmy on his shoulder. "Good. Consider my proposal. I'll pay you double if you stay another week."

Jimmy shrugged. "I can use the money. All right, if you'll help me find Heidi."

The owner said, "I'll see what I can do."

Jimmy walked onto the stage, sat on the stool, and related a few kind words of his recollection of John Lennon. He then spoke to the audience. "Here's a song that I want to dedicate to someone I knew, and I hope someday she'll hear it."

He proceeded to play *No Reply* and near the end of the song a couple walked into the restaurant. Jimmy didn't recognize the man, but the woman seemed familiar. Her face with its soft and gentle features complimented by shoulder length blond hair had every man and even some of the women turning their heads.

Brushing the snow from her coat, she then removed it revealing a bright red sweater underneath.

When Jimmy saw the sweater and took a second look at the woman's face. He knew who she was. He started playing another John Lennon song, *Yes It Is*.

#

The man who accompanied the woman into the restaurant roared at her, "Sit down!"

The woman rolled her eyes and reluctantly took a seat at a table.

A server walked up to their table and asked, "What can I get for you?"

"I'll have a Bud, and keep 'em coming. What do you want?" the man stared at his date.

She looked up at the server. "Just a ginger ale, it won't be long before I'm out of here."

The man laughed. "Yeah, bring her a large soda. She ain't going nowhere."

The server nodded and walked away.

The woman at the table pleaded, "Maxwell, don't do this. I want to go home. I told you we're done."

Maxwell laughed. "Why, what's the matter?"

"What's the matter?" the woman shook her head. "Let's see, pick Anna, Michelle, or Sadie for starters."

"Hey, they don't mean anything to me," Maxwell said.

The woman's voice grew louder, "You cheated on me and I heard that you're still seeing Sadie."

Maxwell pounded his fist on the table. "Hey, get this straight. You and I are not married."

"But we're engaged. How can I trust you when we're married if I can't trust you now?" the woman asked.

Maxwell rolled his eyes. "Well, thank you girl. Hey, isn't it better I get this out of my system before we get hitched?"

A patron at the next table interrupted their conversation. "Hey, can you keep it down? We're trying to listen to the music."

"Mind your own damn business," Maxwell replied.

The patron started to get up but the glint from a silver handled knife in a leather scabbard on Maxwell's belt was in plain view. The patron backed down as Maxwell smiled and then turned to his fiancée.

Maxwell asked, "Tell me why you feel this way."

"Maxwell, I just want out of this."

He glared at her. "Out of what? We can work it out. You're not going anywhere. We've been together too long to end it now."

The woman took a deep breath. "A little too long, I wish I were back in Connecticut. There was someone there who cared about me."

Maxwell's voice became louder. "Oh, so when did YOU cheat on me? That little cross-country backpack trip you took with Julia a few years ago?"

The woman explained, "I didn't cheat on you. It was just a couple of innocent dates, nothing happened. But the guy I met really seemed to care about me. Not like you." The woman pointed to Jimmy on stage. "The guy even played a Beatles song on his guitar, just like this guy on stage."

Maxwell looked at Jimmy who had just finished *Yes It Is*. "So, why'd you come back to me?"

"I didn't want to break his heart. He was so nice to me."

Maxwell mocked her. "Don't make me puke. So, go ahead, find some freaking hippie like that one up on stage. See how long they keep you around."

#

Jimmy heard Maxwell's last few words. As a rebuttal, he dove into the chords of John Lennon's song, *You're Gonna Lose That Girl* and stepped up the volume on his acoustic/electric.

#

Maxwell's face turned a bright crimson and he looked across the table at a smiling face. "Heidi, what the hell do you want from me?"

Heidi leaned forward. "I want you to leave me alone once and for all before we end up killing each other."

Maxwell stared at the ceiling and then back at Heidi. "Fine, you want a life without me, you got it." He stood up just as the server brought them their drinks. He handed the server a ten-dollar bill. "Have the beer on me." Maxwell stormed away from the table stepped outside and slammed the restaurant door behind him.

Heidi glanced at the stage and started to cry.

Jimmy started singing a new song. "It's been a long time, now I'm coming back home." It was Lennon's song *Wait* and Jimmy looked directly at Heidi the entire time he sang it. She returned Jimmy's stare and realized that he looked familiar even through all that hair.

#

The song ended and Jimmy knew he had been singing to his true love. But there was one more song he wanted to sing. He introduced it to his audience.

"If there is one fitting John Lennon song then it is the following one that I would like to end this set with." Jimmy looked at Heidi. "I especially want to dedicate it to the lovely young lady sitting alone over there."

Jimmy began singing, "There are places I remember, all my life…"

It was the Lennon song *In My Life* and Jimmy sang it with such passion that a tear rolled down his cheek as he sang the ending coda, "In my… life I love you more."

After the song, Jimmy initiated a short prayer for the soul of John Lennon. Amid applause, he announced that he would return to play tomorrow evening. He received a standing ovation and disappeared off stage. As he walked in the back with guitar in hand, Heidi ran up to him.

"Please… wait. I need to speak with you," Heidi said.

Jimmy looked at her. "Hello, Heidi."

A smile broadened across her face. "So, it is you. Jimmy?"

"Yes."

"What are you doing here?"

"I came hoping to find you but didn't know how to reach you."

Heidi kissed Jimmy on the cheek melding her moist lips with Jimmy's tear. "Thank you for being so kind to me. I'm so sorry for what I did to you."

Jimmy put his guitar away. After a moment of silence, he said, "All you had to do was tell me the truth. I would have understood. Maybe we can work it out."

Heidi touched Jimmy's arm. "I didn't want to break your heart. Are you willing to give it another try?"

Jimmy smiled. "I would like that more than anything on heaven or earth."

Heidi looked around and then asked, "What else do you have to do tonight?"

Jimmy said, "Nothing. I'm done here."

The restaurant owner overhead their conversation and joined in. "Hello Heidi."

"Mister Westcott, how are you?"

"I'm fine. I see you two have finally reconciled."

Jimmy noticed Heidi's puzzled look and explained. "I told Mister Westcott that I came here looking for you."

Heidi wrapped her arm around Jimmy. "That's right and he found me. This time I won't let him go."

Mister Westcott smiled. "Jimmy, spend some time with Heidi. You are taking my offer of staying another week, aren't you?"

Jimmy looked at Heidi, smiled, and then as Heidi tightened her grip on his arm he replied, "Yes, I'll stay."

"Good. Are you leaving now?" Mister Westcott asked.

Jimmy looked at Heidi. "It's snowing pretty badly. Instead of trying to get home in this mess, I can offer you my room at the Hotel Jefferson-Clinton. I'll sleep in the lobby."

Heidi said, "It is bad out there. All right, I accept your offer."

Jimmy suggested, "How about we sit and talk in the lobby until you're ready to go to sleep. The night clerk makes a good pot of coffee."

Heidi smiled. "Sure. Let's go. How much time will it take to get to the hotel?"

Mister Westcott butted into the conversation and said, "It won't be long. I'll escort you two outside…it's just a few blocks."

Mister Westcott walked ahead of them and escorted them through the rear door of the restaurant. As the trio approached the street via the alley alongside the building, Jimmy noticed the shape of a man leaning against the brick wall of the building. His coat was pulled over his head. As they approached the man, Jimmy realized it was Heidi's date. He saw the man pull a shiny knife from inside his coat and lunge toward Heidi.

Maxwell screamed, "If I can't have you, then no one can."

Jimmy stepped in front of Heidi and faced her. The sharp sting of a steel knife blade cut into his back. Mister Westcott grabbed Maxwell, wrestled him to the ground, and tore the knife from his hand. Heidi screamed as Jimmy fell prone onto the snow. An ever-growing pool of blood colored nature's white carpet. Restaurant customers leaving the front entrance saw what happened and immediately flagged down a passing police cruiser.

Heidi cried, "No! Jimmy, no."

Jimmy lay on the ground in pain. His lips moved but no words left his mouth. He saw the blood below him, then Mister Westcott twisting Maxwell's hand behind his back while the police officer pulled out a pair of handcuffs. He noticed the onlookers, the concern on their faces, and then he saw himself on the ground. Jimmy realized that he was viewing the entire scene from a distance. A loud noise startled him, and he sensed that he was in a long corridor moving ever so slowly toward a bright light. Nearing the end of the tunnel, he felt a hand reach out and grab him.

#

"Bout time you got off yer plates. Welcome Laddie. I've had bugger all to do all day before you showed up."

Jimmy did a double take as John Lennon, wearing his white suit from the Abbey Road album greeted him with a smile.

"Where am I?" asked Jimmy looking down and seeing that he was still wearing his clothes from the restaurant.

"Blimey! Are you daftie? Better ya ask where yer not."

"Is this heaven?" Jimmy asked.

Lennon laughed at him. "Me being a scouser from way back, I'd say right you are. You ought to see the kipper yer sportin'."

"I died?" Jimmy asked.

"Bloody snookered are ya? Are you going to stand there and talk the hind leg off a donkey? Yes, you died and so did I, earlier than you."

Jimmy shook his head. "No this is wrong. This is so wrong."

John placed his hand on Jimmy's shoulder. "No, this is so tickety-boo up here. I already met Buddy Holly, Hendrix, Morrison, and Janis Joplin. And, me mum, I'll see her too."

Jimmy shook his head. "No, this can't be. I've got to get back."

"Hold on mate, don't talk rubbish. I'm not allowed to throw a benny here. Remember those songs I taught ya? I heard you play some tonight. You done a fine job too. We've got so much time I can teach you more of them."

"Where?" Jimmy asked.

"Right here, Laddie." Lennon pulled a guitar out of nowhere and began to play, *You've Got to Hide Your Love Away*. Then his clothes materialized into the snappy jacket and pressed slacks from the Beatles first Ed Sullivan Show performance. When he got to the harmonica part, he tossed the guitar to Jimmy, pulled a Hohner harmonica from behind Jimmy's ear, and continued the song.

When he finished singing, he told Jimmy to play something. Jimmy started strumming *Imagine*. Impressed, Lennon sat on a stool that materialized out of thin air as a white piano rose out of the ground. Lennon accompanied Jimmy and after the song ended, they embraced.

"Whoa, Laddie! We'll have a wicked fancy time here but I'm a bit knackered. You see, that shot I took to the back tonight still hurts. They told me once I meet my mum then there would be no more pain. Just let me rest."

Jimmy felt more at ease and began to accept his fate. "It does feel different up here. No regret, no sorrow."

"That's right." Lennon paused. "Someday I'll get to see my Yoko and soon you'll see your Heidi up here. Ain't that a fancy change of plans?"

"What do you mean, soon? How do you know about Heidi?" Jimmy asked.

John elaborated. "No offense but she's a real fit Lassie. Oh, I hear stuff up here, future stuff. See, you being up here now leaves her with that killer boyfriend."

Jimmy said, "No, he'll go to jail for what he did to me."

John replied, "Not so fast. Seems there was no one willing to testify against him. Heidi was afraid of him, so she let it be."

"What about Mister Westcott? I saw him hold onto the guy," Jimmy said.

Lennon laughed. "Bollocks! That chap you call Westcott didn't want to get involved in the trial."

Jimmy stared into space as John plucked his Epiphone Casino guitar out of the air. "But that's not right. It can't end up that way," Jimmy said.

"I'm telling you how it is, Laddie. Are ya smoking some wacky backy? If ya know where it is up here, then let me know."

Jimmy asked, "What do you know about that guy who killed me?"

"That wanker, he's a bit Chav. Don't be so all gobsmacked. Everyone knows he deserved Her Majesty's Pleasure, but he serves a reduced sentence because no one testifies, and he tells the judge some porkies. Then gets out, stalks that Lassie of yours, and has a one-sided kerfuffle with her. It's enough to make me absolutely gutted."

"Then what?" Jimmy asked.

Lennon shrugged. It doesn't end up good Laddie."

"I want to go back." Jimmy felt a slight tug from behind. "I have to go back." It grew stronger until Jimmy felt himself moving backward. He looked at Lennon. "I think I'm leaving."

Lennon's facial hair grew and a pair of perfectly round, wire-rim eyeglass frames settled onto his face. When the black leather jacket with its plush collar that he wore the night he died, floated down onto his shoulders, Lennon said, "Yer throwing a spanner in the works, Laddie. You're messing with the plan.

Lennon strapped on his Epiphone Casino guitar and began playing the song *Revolution* as Jimmy hurtled backwards.

"I think I'm leaving!" Jimmy yelled.

"Yes you are, and arse over elbow it looks like to me. Well, cheers anyway. You've been the bee's knees to me while you've been up here. I loved having a chinwag with ya. So, it's not your cards yet, mate. Go back to that girl of yours. I know she loves ya. Be good to that Lassie. Give me a bell the next time you arrive."

Jimmy felt a crushing blow when he reentered his body. He felt the pain inflicted from the stab wound but the coldness of the snow and the darkness of the night were gone. Jimmy felt the warmth of a blanket around him, the sound of a siren, and jostling as if he were being transported somewhere in a hurry. Slowly opening his eyes, he noticed Heidi sitting beside him along with an EMT in the back of an ambulance. Heidi was crying and holding his hand while the EMT compressed his hand against the bandage on Jimmy's back.

"Heidi?" Jimmy painfully tried to communicate with her. He called again and this time she heard him.

"Jimmy, you're alive," Heidi said.

"His vitals are stabilizing," the EMT said. "I think he'll be all right."

"Heidi, I…"

Heidi placed her fingers on Jimmy's lips. "Don't talk. I need you to testify and put that monster away for good. You saved my life. I'll never leave you again."

Jimmy smiled as Heidi began to sing to him.

"In my… life I love you more."

Union Station Angel

They say you know exactly when you are touched by an angel. It may be when we face danger and someone or something not of this world influences the outcome. It may be as subtle as a twisted ankle, a red traffic light, or a squirrel crossing the road causing us to delay our activity for a few seconds or it may be as profound as a missed taxi, train, or plane. Whatever it is we can explain the 'what happened' but the 'why it happened' is lost in our orderly rationalization of events.

It was a windy, overcast mid-January morning, the type of weather inherent with winter's bone-chilling influence. Less than six years after the 911 attacks terrorism was a fading concern. Any sense of our personal vulnerability was more than matched by an 'it could never happen to us' fallacy.

That Saturday morning, the drive into Hartford was uneventful. My wife planned her trip to Maine by long-haul bus and had not forgotten a thing. She's like that, always prepared, never a wasted thought or action. I admire her purpose.

"Think the house will be all right?" I asked.

"I'm sure the girls will protect it," she answered.

In our case 'the girls' were two German shorthaired pointers and one boxer. Unflinchingly loyal, they would bark whenever anything appeared out of the ordinary. As large as they are their intimidation level rises along with their exuberance. They are excellent watchdogs as well as wonderful companions.

"Oh, I missed the road," I said as I stared at the left turn that I should have taken. That would have allowed us to navigate into a large parking lot inside the train station's footprint.

"That's okay. Pull onto the next road and go around the block," my wife said.

I should have listened to her.

I slowed our Toyota 4-Runner to a crawl and took a left onto Union Place, a one-way street. Unable to turn around, I looked for another left to loop back to the parking lot. Then I noticed several metered spots on the left sidewalk right in front of the large brownstone building that was Union Station.

"Think this will be all right?" I asked.

She looked at her watch. "The bus leaves in an hour. I'm sure this is fine."

I pulled into a parking spot and we got out. After throwing a half-dozen quarters into the parking meter, I then went to the back of the car. Grabbing her Spartan sum of luggage was a breeze. A one week's visit with her aunt in Old Town Maine wouldn't require much. Most of their time would be spent sitting and reminiscing, maybe an evening bite to eat at one of the many family restaurants in the area. It was a small-town, blue-collar community. No fancy night spots, no hobnobbing with celebrities or people of influence although we did hear that Stephen King's wife was originally from Old Town.

My wife's aunt was recovering from the loss of her husband just a month earlier in December. A heroic figure, he carved out an extraordinary career in law enforcement.

He joined the Maine State Police in his twenties and, upon graduating from the Police Academy; he accepted a troop assignment patrolling from one city to another. A few years later he was promoted to detective and transferred to a different troop where he remained a detective until his retirement. He took great pride in his work as an investigator and was known by many as a legendary State Police detective.

He was also known by some as a rebel due to his outspoken nature and his decision to sometimes do it his own way, of course within the confines of the law. During his career he trained at Harvard University's Associates in Police Science, the United States Narcotics Bureau, and at the U.S. Department of Treasury and Organized Crime Investigation Training.

He was the senior intelligence officer with the New England Organized Crime Intelligence System and retired from the State Police with the rank of detective sergeant. Upon retirement, he began a career as a private investigator and quickly became known as a premier investigator.

His interrogation motto was "Kill 'em with kindness."

Although standing six-feet four inches tall and being the spitting image of actor James Arness, he had a soft heart for those he loved and cherished and fiercely defended them. Both criminals and despicable characters far and wide would never see that side of him. His scowl alone, his gruff, deep voice, or even the sight of his meat hook hands could force an adversary into compliance.

I remember a story my father-in-law told me. When my wife's uncle was serving as a Maine State Trooper during the 1950s, he once had to transport a prisoner. He stopped by the Connecticut gas station where my father-in-law was working. He got out of his cruiser, left the prisoner in the vehicle, and went inside the building.

One of the gas station attendants walked up to the passenger side of the car and spoke to the prisoner. "You're not handcuffed. Why don't you just get out and run?"

The prisoner looked up at the attendant and said, "And how far do you think I'd get? Did you see the hands on that cop?"

When I first met him years earlier, I knew he was special. An intimidating man, he was really a jokester, a kidder. He liked to pull the wool over people's eyes and have a laugh over the most mundane and common things. Perhaps it was his way of lightening the air. Letting others know not to take life so seriously especially when with friends and to be happy with what you have and with those around you. All I knew was that I respected him and felt comfortable in his presence. I believe that he truly loved his niece, my wife, and was happy that we had each found one another. I remember the jokes they shared especially regarding moose sightings.

"Come on up to Maine and I'll show you a real live moose," he often boasted to her.

So, she did. He drove her out into the backwoods of Millinocket one year looking for moose but nary was one to be found. Then as if to counter his infectious humor, my wife would mail him anything resembling a moose. Greeting cards, stuffed animals, buttons, just anything with the face or body of a moose would get mailed to him for a laugh.

Looking at the station's gallery of front windows with the clouds reflected in their glare, we climbed the steps, walked inside, and crossed the expansive lobby. My mind photocopied the marbled walls and maroon-tiled, uncluttered shiny floor. Down a few steps to the bus terminal, we approached the desk and ordered the round-trip ticket. Then we waited. The crowd of travelers ebbed and flowed with the arrival and departure of busses associated with various destinations.

When the bus to Bangor, Maine finally pulled into one of

the dozen or so parking spots outside the bus terminal, I led the way carrying my wife's lone piece of luggage.

"I wish you a safe trip," I said.

My wife laughed. "My angels will take care of that."

She believed wholeheartedly in angels and although I also believed in spiritual forces the fact that they can interact with us on this earthly plane in an ongoing, daily basis seemed like a stretch to me. I always felt that if we placed ourselves into situations then it was up to us to get ourselves out. Nothing else would or could do our bidding. We controlled our own destiny.

We walked up to the bus, but the driver closed the door. Not ready for new passengers…more waiting. There were dozens of people lined up against the outside wall, all presumably waiting for their bus. Then, later the door to the bus opened once again and the driver stood outside. Passengers approached and one by one were admitted onboard. My wife took the carryon luggage from me, hugged, and then kissed me goodbye, walked onto the bus, and found a seat by a window.

Some people who waiting along with me left when their friends or relatives boarded. I stayed longer, until the bus was ready to leave. Close to thirty minutes must have elapsed. I stood alone against the wall of the building. When the bus left, I breathed a sigh and made my way back into the terminal.

I remember passing the front desk and then up the steps toward the lobby. My peripheral vision caught a glimpse of someone to my right. I dared not look, not in the city. As I crossed the lobby, I caught sight of the person following alongside me in stride as we both headed for the glass front doors. Opening one of those doors, I entered a tiny vestibule. Noticing a young man who appeared to be in his late twenties leaning with his back against the wall, I reached for the door knob to exit the station.

The young man said, "Excuse me sir, can you give me a ride to my car. It's stuck on the Interstate."

I surveyed him more closely. Scruffy, sandy hair, a blemished face, a tattered gray sweatshirt, and beat-up blue jeans with random holes here and there telegraphed more than I needed to know.

An emphatic 'no' was all I said and then bounded down the stairs. As I headed for the parked Toyota 4-Runner, I looked back. The sandy-haired youngster had left the station and was making his way down the steps. Another young person, just a bit older with a dark complexion exited the front doors and joined his companion. I realized what was happening. Reaching the car, I pulled the keys from my pocket and tried to unlock the car door. I fumbled with the lock and dropped the keys into the gutter. Bending to pick them up, I heard the older youth shout to me.

"Give me your wallet and your keys."

He stepped forward and pulled a knife with a six-inch blade from under his jacket. Waving it in a threatening manner with his other arm outstretched, he again demanded, "Give me the keys."

The word 'no' barely escaped my lips above a whisper. I flinched as the man's arm thrust forward and the blade drove deep into my midsection. The pain doubled me over and then increased in intensity when he quickly ripped the knife out of the wound. I dropped to my knees and then fell to one side. The blood saturated first my clothing and then the sidewalk.

I felt someone rifle through my pockets. First my wallet was removed, then my keys. I saw them being lifted away. I distinctly remember a laugh, a clap, then a car door open, then another, and our Toyota being driven away. I lay there bleeding, my last everythings slowly leaving this world.

#

But is that what really happened that Saturday morning or is it what could have happened? What could have happened if it weren't for angels…for my wife's special angel?

Oh, everything I explained is true from arriving in Hartford up until meeting that sandy-haired youngster in the vestibule of Union Station and the two men bounding down the steps after me. What really happened after that is subject to conjecture. The physical aspects are easy to explain. My eyes saw what happened and I can describe them most vividly. But does the physical always explain the why things happen? Why it happened the way it did is the mystery that we can never explain.

#

The young man said, "Excuse me sir, can you give me a

ride to my car. It's stuck on the Interstate."

I surveyed him more closely. Scruffy, sandy hair, a blemished face, a tattered gray sweatshirt, and beat-up blue jeans with random holes here and there telegraphed more than I needed to know.

An emphatic 'no' was all I said and then bounded down the stairs. As I headed for the parked Toyota 4-Runner, I looked back. The sandy-haired youngster had left the station and was making his way down the steps. Another young person, just a bit older with a dark complexion exited the front doors and joined his companion. I realized what was happening. Reaching the car, I pulled the keys from my pocket and tried to unlock the car door. I fumbled with the lock and looked back. The two men had taken a few steps toward my car but then stopped, turned back, and stood at the bottom of the station steps. One pulled out two cigarettes, lit them, and they shared a smoke.

When I heard the squawk of a two-way radio, I glanced up and caught sight of two EMT officers sitting in a parked emergency van across the street within a stone's throw of my car. Their windows were partially rolled down and the red flashing lights on their roof reflected off the windows of nearby buildings. The officers seemed to be reviewing a clipboard and speaking via radio with their command center.

I opened my car door, got in, turned on the ignition, and pulled out of the parking spot. As I drove away, I looked through my rear-view mirror and noticed the two young men, eyes peeled watching me leave.

Why did it happen, you ask? Why didn't the first version of this event which I described most clearly become reality?

You see, on that windy day in mid-January, on a mostly barren street in Hartford Connecticut, my wife's special angel was watching over me. An angel that stood six-feet four-inches tall, resembled James Arness, and had a soft heart for those he loved, cherished, and fiercely defended.

*** END ***

www.ingramcontent.com/pod-product-compliance
Lightning Source LLC
Chambersburg PA
CBHW060418050426
42449CB00009B/2011